Classic Land Rovers still inhabit all corners of the globe Shira Klasmer Photography

A CELEBRATION
OF LAND ROVERS

Whatever the reason for your attraction to classic Land Rovers, you're bound to find something of interest between the pages of our 2024 Yearbook.

The team at Classic Land Rover magazine has paged through the past two years of articles and features – and in some cases even further back – to select some of our favourite stories to share with you. They cover adventure travel, restorations, vehicle preparation and even an electric conversion, which is increasingly becoming a talking point among enthusiasts.

In addition, we've sourced 14 pages of new content because there's never a shortage of stories to tell on what owners and their Land Rovers are getting up to.

It's always been the sense of adventure Land Rovers exude that appeals to me. From early on, pioneering explorers recognised the role these farm machines could play in unlocking some of the remotest regions of our planet. It's no wonder then that Land Rover and the Camel Trophy would become synonymous with one another through the 1980s and 1990s. And, of course, no yearbook would be complete without a Trophy vehicle, in this case a Ninety used in Borneo in 1985 by the Italian team.

Incredibly, classic Land Rovers several

> ## 'Pioneering explorers recognised the role these farm machines could play'

decades old are still taking their owners on adventures, be it a simple weekend getaway or travel across continents. In many cases they were rescued from behind barns or in fields and then lovingly restored.

Sometimes the restoration was completed to the high quality shown in our feature on pages 72-77, or done to keep the patina effect (see pages 58-62). Whichever appeals to you, we need to keep these pieces of automotive history running, but whether that includes going as far as a conversion to electric power is a debate for another day. However, it is an issue many of us may be faced with in the coming years. For London resident Yosi Romano, it was a no brainer. You can read more about his reasons on pages 40-44.

Enjoy the read.

Andrew Stone
CLR Editor

CLASSIC LAND ROVER MAGAZINE
YEARBOOK 2024
ISBN: 9781802829365
Editor: Andrew Stone
Senior editor, specials: Roger Mortimer
Email: roger.mortimer@keypublishing.com
Cover design: Steve Donovan
Design: Ros Woodham
Advertising Sales Manager: Brodie Baxter
Email: brodie.baxter@keypublishing.com
Tel: 01780 755131
Advertising Production: Becky Antoniades
Email: rebecca.antoniades@keypublishing.com

SUBSCRIPTION/MAIL ORDER
Key Publishing Ltd, PO Box 300, Stamford, Lincs PE9 1NA
Tel: 01780 480404
Subscriptions email: subs@keypublishing.com
Mail Order email: orders@keypublishing.com
Website: www.keypublishing.com/shop

PUBLISHING
Group CEO and Publisher: Adrian Cox

Published by
Key Publishing Ltd, PO Box 100, Stamford, Lincs, PE9 1XQ
Tel: 01780 755131 **Website:** www.keypublishing.com

PRINTING
Precision Colour Printing Ltd, Haldane,
Halesfield 1, Telford, Shropshire TF7 4QQ

DISTRIBUTION
Seymour Distribution Ltd, 2 Poultry Av., London EC1A 9PU
Enquiries Line: 02074 294000

We are unable to guarantee the bona fides of any of our advertisers. Readers are strongly recommended to take their own precautions before parting with any information or item of value, including, but not limited to money, manuscripts, photographs, or personal information in response to any advertisements within this publication.

KEY

P52 Collector nets Camel Trophy Ninety from Borneo
P30 How a former British Army Snatch landed in Ukraine
P106 The 'new' Discovery HC is an impressive vehicle
P100 1969 Series IIA fire engine camper in Europe
Uber-cool resto-mod Series IIA P06

First production Land Rover takes to the road again P58

Two Land Rover Minervas from Brussels to India P78

Land Rover and the royal family P24

SUBSCRIBE AND SAVE!
Make great savings when you subscribe to Classic Land Rover today
See page 29 for all special offers

CONTENTS

CLASSIC
LAND ROVER

California Dreamin'

Land Rover and
V8 engine specialist
Leon Attenborough has
created petrolhead
Wayne Hayhurst's dream
vehicle – an uber-cool
resto-mod Series IIA

WORDS **EMRYS KIRBY**
PICTURES **GARRY STUART**

**This vehicle has real presence
and sounds awesome**

The classic Land Rover scene has changed significantly over the past decade and noticeably over the 100 issues of CLR that I have contributed to. Classic Land Rovers have come of age and have passed from a niche hobby to mainstream cool.

It's fair to say that values have risen with this trend and the broadening of the scene has also created two growing trends – the better-than-new-concours 'rivet counter' restoration and the 'resto-mod'.

The latter has become well known through several high-profile Instagram pages like Coolnvintage in Lisbon, Falcon Design Germany and ACH Classics in Silverstone.

In short, a resto-mod is a fully restored vehicle that has been modified either for ease of use, for performance improvements, to support a personal lifestyle or built to personal taste.

It's not necessarily about functionality but creating a beautiful vehicle, a piece of craftsmanship and dare I say, a piece of automotive art. Now I know these vehicles are not to everybody's taste, especially if you still think of Land Rovers as being works' hacks to be repaired on a tight budget, but the scene is broad enough to allow people who are less cost-conscious to commission something stunning.

The value of these vehicles cannot be easily determined by marketplace comparisons because it's about commissioning talented people to build your bespoke, dream vehicle. Quality costs; not just because you're paying for craftsmanship but the amount of time to fully strip, restore, modify and handcraft a bespoke vehicle can be phenomenal.

Leon Attenborough from the Ribble Valley area of Lancashire has just finished this stunning resto-mod IIA dream build for his good customer and now very proud owner Wayne Hayhurst.

Leon is one of those multi-talented people who can turn his hand to any restoration job. That is every single task and bespoke fabrication on this vehicle from repairing the chassis and building the engine to fabricating the highly bespoke exhaust pipes.

Leon has a background not only in all generations of Land Rover but highly accurate fabrication in motorsport having worked for well-known roll cage manufacturer PP Cages in Kelbrook, Lancashire.

He has lots of experience building highly tuned Rover V8s and Ford BDA engines for Paul Gardner Race Engines in Scorton near Lancaster. In addition, he is heavily involved in tractor pulling and competes successfully in his Bowland Raptor, a Ford 810-based tractor with a highly tuned engine, another of his special bespoke builds.

Wayne Hayhurst has been a long-standing customer of Leon's – he has an enviable collection of interesting and rare cars that Leon has fettled and restored over the years. He comes from Ribble Valley farming stock but now runs a business in investment and wealth management.

He has grown up with Land Rovers on the family farm and bought a Defender 110 XS towards the end of classic production. Land Rovers are very much in his blood. He's not a newcomer to the scene, it's just that he has the financial clout to have a trusted and talented person build his dream vehicle.

The commission to build the resto-mod IIA was the development of casual conversations between Wayne and Leon and they worked through a series of possible ideas. Inspiration came from Coolnvintage-style vehicles and the famous Golden Rod, a yellow 1966 Series IIA that was built in California for the Rover Motor Company of North America as the original test vehicle for the Rover V8.

There is certainly a Golden State vibe with this vehicle – you look at it and cannot help but think of adventuring in the sunshine and driving down to golden sandy beaches. Not only that, it's finished in Bahama Gold, an original Range Rover colour.

The basis for the restoration is a 1968

'It's not necessarily about functionality but creating a beautiful vehicle'

Series IIA that had originally been used on a shooting estate in Scotland: it came with a hardtop that had been fitted with a personnel hatch to shoot through.

The commission was a perfectly timed job for Leon to keep him busy throughout the Covid lockdown period. He was also aware that with the growing appetite for resto-mod vehicles, this could well be a testbed and advertising vehicle that would showcase his skill, vision and attention to detail.

Given his background in motorsport fabrication, he understandably takes a great deal of pride in his welding skills and decided that the original chassis should be repaired to new condition.

A new chassis would be an easier option but Leon decided he liked the authenticity of keeping the original. Fairly extensive repairs were necessary, especially to the rear and underside of the chassis rails and outriggers. There were previous poor repairs to rectify and the usual rear crossmember replacement was required. Now you really cannot see any evidence of the joins or repairs, the true sign of top-quality restoration work and it's finished off in gloss black.

The axles were treated to a full overhaul - the rear axle case had corroded badly and required new strengthening gussets. These were bolted to the rolling chassis with a set of Santana specification multi-leaf springs.

While parabolic springs are common on many modified Land Rovers, Leon chose these because good quality multi-leaf springs don't suffer from 'torque wrap' the way thinner parabolics can, an important consideration given that the plan was to fit a modified Rover V8.

Not only that, good multi-leaf springs do provide a good ride and handling performance as long as they are in good condition. Damping is looked after by

Bespoke twin exhaust gives a distinctive burble

Ignition amplifier and aluminium header tank on the bulkhead

Britpart Cellular Dynamic long travel shock absorbers which give a fantastic ride – perfectly matched to the vehicle's increased performance.

The steering has all-new ball joints and Leon decided to fit a lower ratio One Ton/six-cylinder-type steering box to make it easier to turn the wheel with larger tyres.

The vehicle rolls on 235 85 R16 Cooper Discoverer ATs mounted on new, tubeless Britpart 16x8 large offset rims (part number DA2694).

This is a cost-effective, modern version of the old One Ton or Forward Control-style wheels that are highly sought after at the moment.

These come in black primer but Leon sprayed them gloss black as a strong contrast to the bodywork. Braking is looked after by twin leading shoe 11in drums on the front and 10in on the back, just like a late model Series III SWB.

With Leon being a Rover V8 specialist, this vehicle was always going to have something special under the bonnet. It's fitted with a fettled 3.9 'serpentine belt' Discovery EFI engine (officially referred to as the 4.0 engine) but it's running a Weber/Edelbrock 500 carb.

It was only removed from the donor vehicle to fit a TDV6 engine and was a known good unit. Leon fitted new rings and a high-lift Kent cam along with a Range Rover flywheel, drilled for a heavy-duty Series III clutch, for better torque characteristics.

It runs a distributor and electronic ignition with a neat ignition amplifier (as used on Paul Gardner BDA race engines) on the bulkhead.

Specially fabricated engine mount brackets pick up on the original 2,286cc chassis mounting points and raise the crankshaft line slightly. The oil filter housing, which usually points perilously close to the front diff, has been machined off.

It's now fitted with unions and pipes run to a remote Mocal filter header on the passenger inner wing. Cooling is looked after by a new aluminium cored 2,286cc radiator but Leon has fitted a new alloy remote header tank, in addition, there is a cooling fan fitted behind the grille.

He has also retained the original water pump bypass system, ensuring correct coolant flow and reducing the possibility of airlocks. The engine is fitted to a standard rebuilt Series III LT76 gearbox running through a rebuilt transfer box to standard

Discovery 3.9 serpentine belt engine with Weber 500 carb

'You look at it and cannot help but think of adventuring in the sunshine and driving down to golden sandy beaches'

The classic resto-mod scene is growing, inspired by CoolNvintage (and now Leon!)

From left, creator Leon Attenborough and proud owner Wayne Hayhurst

This vehicle just oozes Golden State sunshine cool

Wayne is delighted with the standard of this build

ratio Series IIA differentials. A Fairey overdrive improves the overall gearing for higher-speed driving.

Leon rebuilt the original bulkhead but this also had to be modified to accommodate the extra width of the V8 exhaust manifolds. This involved trimming the passenger footwell and widening the centre panel.

Again, the true sign of quality workmanship is that the modification is not obvious. Leon was lucky enough to have access to a full professional painting booth and top-quality spray guns in a neighbouring unit. The finish is spectacular and Wayne's choice of Bahama Gold is bold but somehow has a real classic air about it.

The body cappings, grille and windscreen frame were re-galvanized. As a little quirk from standard, Leon refitted the top side cappings with stainless cap head set screws – it's different and very much in keeping with a resto-mod.

The Lucas L488 glass rear lamps came from Charles Emberton and while they are not 'age-correct' for a 1968 vehicle they look perfect on a resto-mod and ooze a quality that you don't get with the later plastic lenses.

Leon is now in a position to take on more commissions. To find out more, check out his Instagram @leonattenborough, email: leonattenborough@gmail.com or telephone: 07861 792994.
The Land Rover even has an Instagram account – check out @landys2a

The rear tub is lined with iroko wood and this required the fuel filler cover to be shortened to fit – it sounds simple but with multiple dimensions to reform, it was time-consuming to make it look just right.

The rear tub also sports a heavy-duty seatbelt bar: Leon's own design and built using the high-tech machinery at PP Cages.

Further attention to detail can be found on the dash. Leon modified a wiper motor cover to house auxiliary gauges and switches to the right of the main dash. He also modified a Mini steering column binnacle to house the indicator switch. It fits remarkably well and just adds a touch of class that also looks at home with the Exmoor Trim wooden rim steering wheel.

Beyond the stunning golden hue of the vehicle, you'll probably hear it coming before you see it. This is thanks to the bespoke, wide-bore stainless steel twin exhausts that Leon fabricated.

These exit through twin EFI manifolds and follow a high-level path to exit just aft of the passenger door. The pipes are deliberately imbalanced to create a very distinctive burble, almost Harley-Davidson-like, as requested by Wayne.

One of the vital factors in creating a resto-mod is how it makes the driver feel and this visceral engine note is awesome. In a world where electric cars are likely to become more common, this is a last hurrah for the joys of internal combustion. **CLR**

Glorious iroko wood in the load bay

Fantastic details on the dashboard – note bespoke auxiliary dash and Mini binnacle

Rated
Trustpilot
"Excellent"
Based on over 25,000 reviews

EMPIRE ADVENTURE

A groundbreaking circumnavigation of the world in 1957/8

WORDS **TOBY SAVAGE** PHOTOS **BRISTOL FOSTER, ROBERT BATEMAN, STUART LONGAIR, WILL BURROWS**

Planning any ambitious adventure by Land Rover required a similar amount of tenacity, funds and ambition 65 years ago today as it does today. The one big advantage for some travellers back then, was that many of the more remote countries belonged to a colonial empire and could be crossed with little more than a passport and a letter of transit. Two suitably ambitious young Canadians were biologist Bristol Foster and wildlife artist Robert Bateman.

Robert later remembered laughing in 1956 when Bristol called him up and asked if he fancied driving around the world. Bristol had just finished a master's degree in biology and Robert had finished a degree in geography and was by then teaching.

However, they were both single and unhindered by commitments, so the pair sat down with a simple high school atlas and planned their trip. They agreed on equatorial Africa, and northern India because it led to Nepal, the Himalayas, Burma, Thailand, Malaya and across to Australia. To add gravitas to the 'Bateman Foster Expedition' it would be promoted as a journey of scientific value collecting samples for the Royal Ontario Museum.

Fortunately, Bristol's father was an eminent Toronto businessman and agreed to help with the finances if Bristol and Robert put $2,000 each into the fund. The pair worked hard and saved as much money as they could to get them started. Many letters were sent to prospective sponsors and research stations along the route which might be in a position to offer work to help fund the trip. They also had to learn about the practicalities of driving, living in and maintaining a vehicle in the field, as they aspired to be driving through some of the most remote areas on the planet.

They set their goal on a LWB Land Rover, with a custom-built body to offer comfort and space while on the road. Starting with a new rolling chassis, the work was carried out by the Pilcher company in England, which adapted one of its ambulance bodies to fit the Land Rover chassis.

Kicking up the dust in the Australian outback. By now halfway around the world

Subsequent restoration in 2013 showed that they were learning on the job as each side of the rear body showed different design and construction methods! The result was just what the two men wanted and it even had a unique turret hatch cut into the roof, so they could observe wild animals from the safety of the car.

Bristol flew to England for a full training course in Land Rover maintenance at Solihull and off-road driving skills were learnt on the company's test track before Robert joined him for the official handover from Land Rover.

From there they embarked on a vehicle shakedown trip to Scotland, christening the Land Rover 'The Grizzly Torque' and writing

'They also had to learn about the practicalities of driving, living in and maintaining a vehicle in the field'

the name above the windscreen. Then as now, it is only through real experience that a Land Rover becomes ready for an expedition.

Certain items you presume are essential are discarded in favour of simpler things that were not initially thought of. The trip to Scotland fine-tuned their requirements

and with that, they set off to explore three continents. The 'Bateman Foster Expedition' went through much of Central Africa where highlights included meeting a tribe of Mbuti Pygmies, scaling the highest peaks near the headwaters of the Nile and getting close to the big game out in the bush where they were most grateful for their turret hatch to aid safe observation. Along the way, Robert painted small pictures on the side of the Land Rover showing where they had travelled and the sights they had seen.

From Africa they headed across northern India, where they suffered their only accident, laying the Land Rover on its side to avoid a cyclist on a narrow mountain road. Luckily passengers from a passing bus leapt

A slight mishap. Swerving to avoid an erratic cyclist in India The Grizzly Torque fell onto its side

Luckily a passing bus saw the accident and the passengers got out to help right the stricken Land Rover

out to assist and righted the stricken vehicle.

The pair then continued their journey through Nepal, Burma, Thailand, Malaya and eventually to Australia from where The Grizzly Torque was shipped back to Canada after a 14-month, 60,000km journey.

Once back in Toronto, Bristol drove it to Vancouver to complete his PhD, using The Grizzly Torque to explore the wilderness of British Columbia. The Land Rover was then sold to a fellow academic who intended to carry out research in Texas and as far as anybody knew that was the last that was heard of it.

One can only speculate that like so many other old Land Rovers with little value, it fell into disrepair and was parked up in a field and forgotten.

Decades later, Canadian Land Rover enthusiast, Stuart Longair bought a job lot of four Series One Land Rovers and restoration of the other three took priority over the quirky ambulance-bodied LWB.

It was not until eight years later, in 2014, that his attention was drawn to various photos on the internet about a Series One, 107in, that had circumnavigated the world back in 1957/8. Stuart had unwittingly bought The Grizzly Torque.

The identity of this important Series One was confirmed by none other than Bristol Foster, who had not seen it for more than 50 years and a plan was put in place to restore the vehicle in time for the All-British Field Meet in Vancouver in May 2015.

Stuart worked closely with his friend, the restorer Alan Simpson, and carefully dismantled the Land Rover recording every

'It fell into disrepair and was parked up in a field and forgotten'

facet of how it had been designed and built as they realised this was a one-off design. As one would expect, rust had taken its toll on both the chassis and bulkhead, but the bespoke aluminium body was fairly complete, if a little cracked in places. Most parts were at least there to act as a pattern, except a few hinges and other small fittings that had been removed for other projects over the intervening years.

With the Land Rover reduced to many carefully labelled parts, work began on the chassis, which was shot-blasted and then ➲

A PR shot for Fina Petrol, one of the sponsors illustrating the home-from-home setup

A chance encounter with a group of Mbuti Pygmies in the Congo region of Central Africa

Observing a field of ant hills in central Africa

Robert Bateman worked on the paintings that told the story of their travels in a non-lingual way

Mechanical problems were minimal. Here they investigate an issue with the front axle

A feast of fresh crabs eaten in Thailand

The Grizzly Torque is hoisted onto a ship for departure to another continent

Bristol Foster travelled to meet restorer Alan Simpson and confirm that this was indeed their historic Grizzly Torque

One of many features unique to The Grizzly Torque was this turret hatch for observing wildlife

The original Land Rover publicity shot at the Rover factory with mud from the test track still on the tyres

Sadly Bristol and Robert, both keen supporters of the project, were unable to make it to the Vancouver Show, but restorer Alan (peering out of the hatch) and owner Stuart managed to recreate the original Land Rover publicity shot

welded to the steel work table to eliminate any distortion. As usual, the bottom had rotted away completely, along with the dumb irons and outriggers, but there was enough left to make the existing chassis repairable rather than fit a new one. While Alan Simpson and his team got on with the build, Stuart Longair was firing off emails to any suppliers who would be able to provide the many other parts required; engine parts came from Dunsfold Land Rovers here in the UK, tail lights from Australia, a new steering wheel and various 1950s fastenings from the UK.

Alan's next task was to tackle the bulkhead which was the usual latticework of rust and more rust that vaguely resembled the shape of its former self. A jig was made to ensure the restored item would fit the chassis properly and work began.

Each panel had to be fabricated from scratch using other Series One bulkheads for measurements where there was simply nothing left, and online help from The Series One Club forum.

The result is a great testament to patience and tenacity. One of the saddest aspects of the bodywork was that Robert Bateman's paintings along the sides of the Land Rover had been lost forever when a previous owner had stripped the bodywork back to bare aluminium to paint it blue.

On the strength of that, it was again stripped back and the original sand yellow was applied to repaired and restored panels. Meanwhile, parts were arriving from all over the globe; springs, shock absorbers, wheels, original Dunlop Trackgrip tyres and freshly recovered seats were sitting in the workshop waiting to be fitted as various aspects of the build were finished.

With the show in Vancouver just days away decisions on what had priority had to be made and it was decided to present The Grizzly Torque as a 'work in progress', as there were still a few parts missing and time had run out. The show attracted a record attendance of 6,000 visitors and 560 cars and Stuart and Alan were very happy to walk away with the 'Best Debuting Restoration', 'Best in Class' and 'Land Rover Spirit' awards. **CLR**

Stuart Longair filled in details of the Grizzly Torque's recent history: 'It was stored up at Alan Simpson's Ranch and in 2019, survived a forest fire that got to the edge of his property. Then in November, they had a catastrophic flood where Alan was airlifted out at 2:30am and he lost half of his farm to the river. So I consider myself very lucky that all my Rovers survived. I decided to sell it at auction, where it made a six-figure sum and went to an American collector. Robert Bateman first re-did the paintings on small cards. We made transfers and applied them to the sides and then Bateman touched them up himself at the Vancouver International Auto Show in 2016'.

DRIVE THE DREAM

In just its second year, the 'Dakar Classic' category was the perfect challenge for the Vintage Racing Team and its three classic Series IIs

WORDS **CLARE WESTBROOK**
PICTURES **DUŠAN & FRANKIE RANDÝSEK/ ŠTĚPÁN PANCE /**
AS CREDITED ILLUSTRATION **LOUISE LIMB**

The Dakar Rally is the stuff dreams are made of. Exotic destinations, exciting travel, the thrill of racing; a bit of danger, a lot of adventure, and the chance to become part of a legendary event.

You'll know the infamous stories: in 1988, Ari Vatanen's Peugeot 405 T16 was stolen and held to ransom and in 1982, Mark Thatcher, his co-driver, mechanic, and their Peugeot 504 went missing in the Algerian Sahara for six days. But every team has a story to tell; Dušan Randýsek and Štěpán Pance, from two of the three Vintage Racing Team crews, have shared theirs about the 2022 rally.

Like all the best adventures, it started with a spontaneous idea. Dakar veteran Dušan Randýsek flew back from the 2021 Rally determined to compete in the new 'Dakar Classic' category.

He co-opted his friend, Petr, with his son Tomáš as co-driver, on the journey home from the airport! Then Štěpán's brother Albert got involved; and finally, Štěpán stepped in when Albert's original co-driver pulled out. The Vintage Racing Team from the Czech Republic was born! They had

'Like all the best adventures, it started with a spontaneous idea'

fewer than 12 months to prepare; it was already mid-January and the vehicles had to be ready for technical scrutineering in Marseilles at the end of November.

This would be Czech Offroad marathon champion Dušan's sixth Dakar. He's competed on motorcycles, in SSVs (side-by-side vehicles also known as buggies), developed an early model of the Wildcat, and drove the PH-Sport fast assistance truck in 2021.

The Classic was an opportunity to compete in his 1964 Series II, which he's owned since 2010, with his son František (Frankie) at his side. At 18, Frankie was the youngest competitor in the rally. He's currently studying acting, but grew up building cars and racing with his father, and has experience in desert competitions in Tunisia.

Petr and Tomáš were the other father and son crew, driving a 1960 Series II they named The Little Green Land Rover. Despite being an experienced circuit racer, this was Petr's Dakar debut and a very different style of racing altogether. Tomáš has been accompanying him to races and rallies since he was a boy, and has useful experience in restoring classic vehicles.

Brothers Albert and Štěpán were the third crew; experienced competition drivers who love classic cars. Štěpán works for Skoda, Albert works in the family business and they both dreamed of doing the Dakar. The Classic category was perfect: closest to their hearts and their budget. They bought their Land Rover, Cecil, from the Czech Land Rover Club. And Cecil turned out to be the team's problem child.

Cecil is a 1965 Series IIA, bought as a non-runner, so Štěpán and Albert had to do a complete renovation. They wanted to keep it as standard as possible, apart from specific requirements stipulated by FIA rules and the Dakar organisers, plus some practical expedition modifications.

The former included the addition of a roll-cage, racing seats and harnesses, fire extinguishers, electric kill switches and

powerful lights; the latter meant fitting an extra fuel tank, a stronger cooling system for water and oil, an electronic distributor and a Weber carburettor. There were storage modifications too, for camping equipment, tools and spare parts, which all had to be secured properly to prevent them flying around on rough terrain.

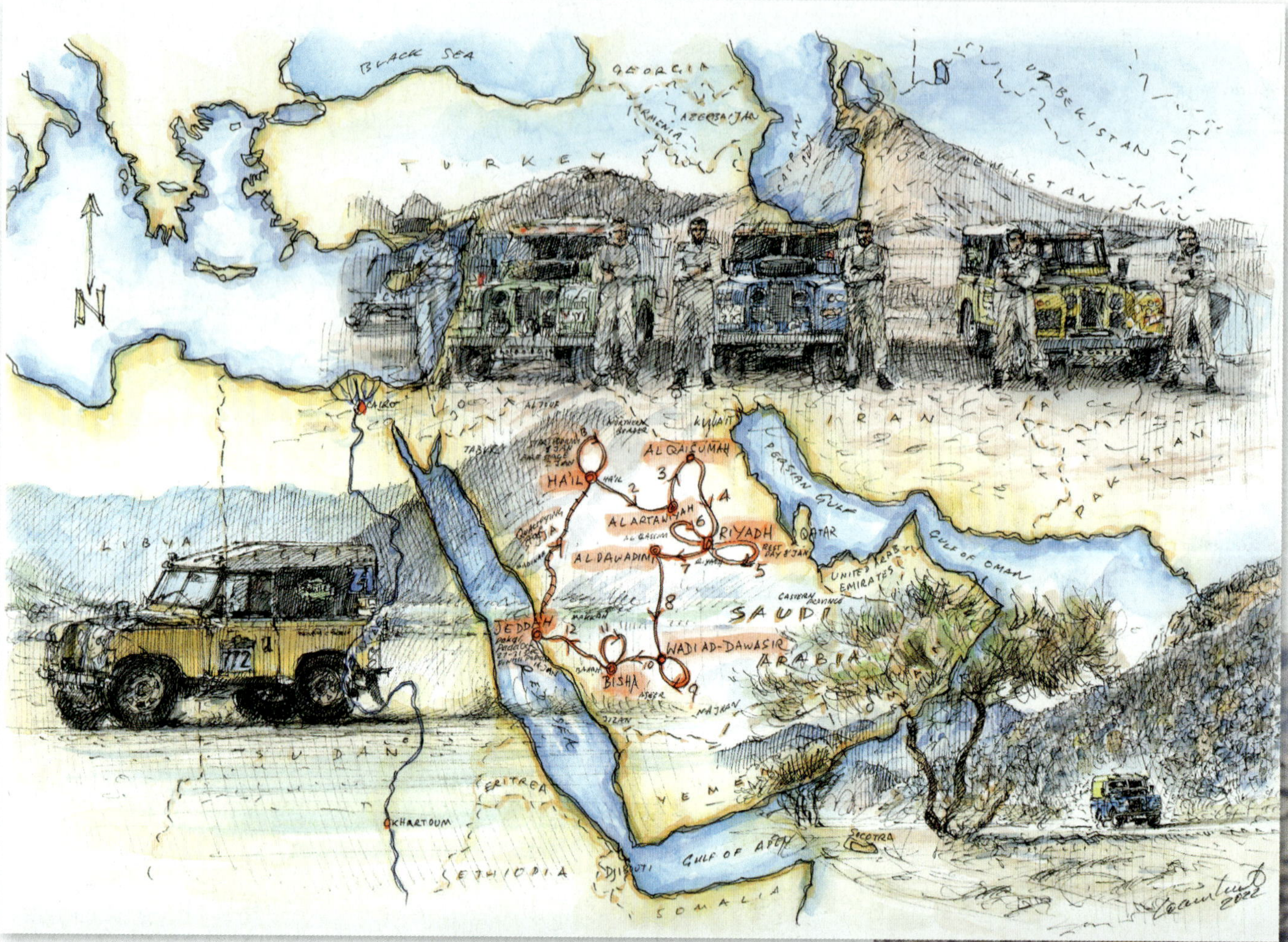

Dušan and Frankie's yellow 1964 Series IIA has the original three-bearing engine, with matching chassis and engine numbers. It was in use, as what Dušan calls "an honest driver", before the event, but still needed complete renovation.

Having decided to run without mechanics or support, the focus had to be on reliability. They spent 1,600 hours bringing 'Ladinek' (Little Vladimir) up to their standards, adding all the safety and regulatory requirements, plus an extra fuel tank, better cooling, and a Roamerdrive overdrive.

There are also two fuel pumps and two coils, so they could switch them quickly if they needed to. Without support mechanics, there wouldn't be any chance of fixing a major issue such as engine or transmission failure, but Dušan and Frankie carried spare differentials, axles, driveshaft, water pump, radiator and steering column; plus a recovery kit including a high lift jack and airbags for lifting.

Cecil, Ladinek and The Little Green Land Rover all passed the technical scrutineering in Marseilles and were loaded onto the transport ship bound for Jeddah. The crews joined the official

Dušan getting down and dirty under his Land Rover

Once the engine stops, there is a great sense of silence and calm in the desert

Czech Dakar flight, organised by Big Shock Racing, and flew directly to Jeddah to be reunited with their Land Rovers.

As they stood at the start, Štěpán and Albert were excited, nervous, full of expectation and a little bit worried. For Dušan, this wasn't a new experience, but it was extra special because he was with Frankie; it was wonderful to be competing alongside his son in his old Land Rover.

The two crews had very different rally

'The Classic was an opportunity to compete in his 1964 Series II, which he's owned since 2010' experiences. Finishing was Dušan's mission, but as he says: "The Dakar has no mercy".

They finished without any major help, though not without issues. The first day was fantastic, they laughed all day, and the Land Rover was fun to drive, although slow.

By day three they were trying to make up time; the small engine and leaf springs were slowing them down; but miraculously, they were too fast arriving at some of the checkpoints!

Days were tough, starting early, driving long distances to the stage start, then the special stage, followed by long distances to the day's finish point. They had problems with overheating fuel and overheating wheel hubs; they bent the axles and broke the flanges; after the first day they were adding oil: "Everywhere and all the time"; and they did the last stage with no front-wheel drive — in fact, they only had one-wheel drive! It was a relief to see the finish ramp.

For Štěpán and Albert, the problems

Rest day (January 8) was anything but restful for the Vintage Racing Team. © A.S.O./Fotop

started on stage two, when their first valve spring broke, leaving them running on three cylinders rather than four. It's such a rare problem on a stock engine that they didn't have a spare, so Štěpán took an Uber to the nearest city and walked around the car workshop area until he found a place full of old cylinder heads.

The owner unearthed some suitable-looking springs and Štěpán bought two, just in case. With the spring replaced, they set the valve clearance and were ready to go; but Cecil had other ideas!

The next day, just before the special stage, another spring broke. Štěpán whipped out his spare and they fitted it at the side of the road in 90 minutes. They missed that special stage, but a few days passed without incident; then the evening before the rest day, yet another spring broke.

The local Land Rover community – namely Faisal and Khalid – came to the rescue, finding a workshop with a full set of matching valve springs which worked perfectly for the rest of the rally.

But the fuel system didn't! Enter Rory – an ex-pat UK Land Rover enthusiast – with an electric fuel pump meant for a Toyota. He drove 400km to the overnight rally bivouac, fitted the pump, and drove 400km back home. Štěpán and Albert cannot thank him enough. After all the problems, getting to the finish line felt like a huge victory for them; it was a childhood dream come true.

Despite all the problems, they enjoyed the rally. Štěpán was surprised by the beauty and variety of the desert landscape. They

Reaching the finish line was a dream come true.
© Ricardo Leizer

IF YOU'RE TEMPTED!

The Dakar Rally covers some 8,500km, including 4,500km of special stages, in 13 gruelling driving days, with one rest day in the middle.

To apply for entry to the Dakar you must...

- Be aged 18 years or over;

- Hold an International FIA/FIM Cross-Country Rally licence; and

- Have participated in one FIA/FIM World Championship event or any other event on the FIA/FIM calendar or your national calendar.

The organiser reserves the right to refuse entry to any competitor who does not have a minimum of recent experience in competitive racing or the physical capabilities necessary to compete in the Dakar.

had a couple of scary moments, but their most memorable was during a three-hour breakdown: the sun was setting, and Štěpán and Albert had the chance to simply enjoy the silence, calmness and greatness of the desert.

For Dušan and Frankie, it was fun from beginning to end, though the tiredness was tough. Travelling and racing with his son made it very special for Dušan and he would do it again.

However if you want to win, he says you should take a V8 Range Rover on coil springs and some support mechanics.

He also says: "You only live once. Don't wait too long; make it possible and do it while you can". **CLR**

Petr and Tomáš motoring through the desert on Stage 1B, January 2, 2022. © A.S.O./Fotop

BELOW: With Cecil on the recovery truck (twice), Štěpán and Albert phoned around to find solutions

CROY TEC
Keeping a Legend in trim
Croytec are dedicated to developing products with style and quality
2003 20th ANNIVERSARY 2023
DESIGNED & MADE IN BRITAIN
We give form to our components by machining detail into them with chamfered edges and rounded corners, under cuts, engraving and much more. We take time with care and attention to detail to ensure we deliver quality products. Our products have become a feature to many Land Rovers worldwide.
Alongside our aluminium interior and exterior trim range, our Special Order Service offers leather trim which can be designed to your requirements incorporating our colour anodised parts, to give you the ultimate Enhanced by Croytec Defender.
www.croytec.co.uk | +441691791349

DUCKWORTH PARTS
Duckworth Motor Group is a family-owned and run official Jaguar Land Rover Retailer, with over 40 years of experience in the motor trade.
Get the part you need for your classic Land Rover
Test our 40+ years knowledge of working with Classic Land Rovers and talk to an expert directly 01673 844722
OWJ 188
www.duckworthparts.co.uk
Racecourse Garage, Willingham Road, Market Rasen LN8 3RE T: 01673 844722

The Royals

AND THEIR 'REGAL' LAND ROVERS

Neil Huband investigates the relationship between
the royal family and Land Rover

WORDS **NEIL HUBAND** PICTURES **AS CREDITED**

On May 21, 1942, it was an overcast day when King George VI and Queen Elizabeth had their first real experience of a utilitarian go-anywhere 4x4, an experience that would lead to a lifelong appreciation of one of Britain's most iconic motor companies, Land Rover.

It was the day that our royal family began its long and fond relationship with sometimes basic but robust, practical and characterful off-road vehicles. The wartime King and his Queen were being given a demonstration of a new kind of vehicle that would spawn a whole range of workmanlike off-roaders including, a few years later, the nation's favourite, the British Land Rover.

The royal couple had been invited to a demonstration of the skills of the newly formed Southern Command Airborne Forces. They saw troop-carrying gliders and watched and met paratroopers and spoke to the women who packed parachutes. At the end of the visit, they were driven away in a brand new Ford GP 'air portable' Jeep.

The King sat in the back under the rough canvas and the Queen sat, beaming, in the front passenger seat as they were driven off in this uncomfortable, noisy, draughty little vehicle, sporting a Pegasus pennant on its bonnet and an airborne logo on its slat grille.

As the war years rolled on, the royal couple were to ride in quite a few more Jeeps at various inspections and other events and, judging by the photographs, they always enjoyed those morale-boosting visits. They had several armoured Humber 4x4 cars for their use in case Hitler invaded. These were never liked and never used.

Throughout their lives, the King and Queen enjoyed the peace, and privacy they could enjoy in the country, in particular their times at Balmoral and Sandringham. Shooting parties and equestrian events were always popular too.

It seemed only fitting then, that in 1948 after The Wilks Brothers had produced their own version of the Jeep, the aluminium-bodied Land Rover, the King should be presented with the 100th vehicle off the production line.

By all accounts, it was very much welcomed and well used, in and around the Balmoral estate in particular. Many years later, while visiting Royal Deeside, Prince Charles was delighted to see his grandfather's Series One, 'resting peacefully' in a garage in Ballater.

This gift marked the beginning of what is now a 75-year relationship between the Land Rover marque and our royal family.

During those war years, the then Princess Elizabeth learned the practical side of motoring as she trained with the Women's Auxiliary Territorial Service based at Camberley in Surrey.

It is said she learned not only how to change a wheel on an Austin Tilly but also how to strip an engine and carry out general maintenance. She also learned to drive Austin K2 ambulances.

Sharing her mother's love of equestrian events and the countryside in general, it was only natural that she too developed an affinity for the then very basic Land Rover and went on to own and drive many different versions before she died in 2022.

By 1951 Land Rover had won its first Royal Warrant as a supplier of vehicles to the royal family with mainly soft top Series One models in use at Balmoral, Sandringham and Windsor. ➲

'This gift marked the beginning of what is now a 75-year relationship between the Land Rover marque and our royal family'

The Duke Of Edinburgh's coffin, borne on the Land Rover he helped to design. Crown Copyright

Prince Philip, Duke of Edinburgh seated on the roof of a Land Rover pointing out competitors at the Badminton Horse Trials to the Queen who is watching through binoculars, April 20, 1968. Jim Gray/Keystone/Hulton Archive/Getty Images

Queen Elizabeth and Prince Philip in Fiji during their royal tour, February 1977 Serge Lemoine / Getty Images

The first state/ceremonial Series One State IV
British Motor Museum

The first state/ceremonial Range Rover State 1
British Motor Museum

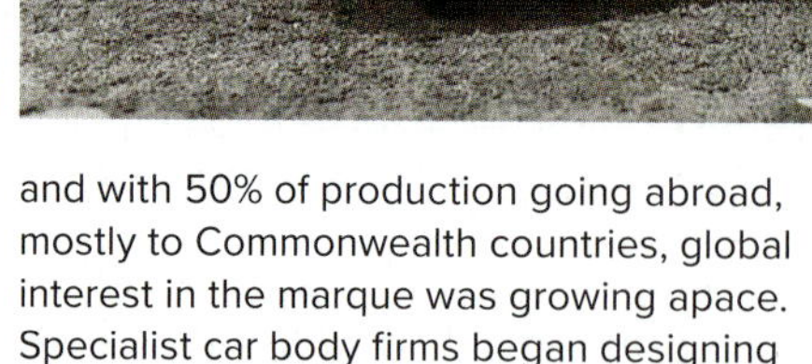

The Queen and Prince Philip wave to the crowds in Australia Wikicommons / State Library of Queensland, Australia

These workaday but capable utility vehicles, that could be used either by farm managers or the 'bosses' on a shooting party, were in stark contrast to the limousines that frequently carried the senior royals to big occasions. But there was still rationing and hardship in those early years after the war and practicality rather than opulence was more appropriate for that time.

This first Royal Warrant was followed by two more over the years and Land Rover became one of the very few companies to hold three Royal Warrants, one each for Queen Elizabeth, Prince Philip and later, Prince Charles.

Gradually the Land Rover replaced the well-used wartime Jeep for HM Forces and with 50% of production going abroad, mostly to Commonwealth countries, global interest in the marque was growing apace. Specialist car body firms began designing special models for the rich and famous.

Following the coronation, a Series One was customised for the Queen's State Review. This 86in was the first of the bespoke royal Land Rovers and was known as the 'State IV'. The body had a rear platform with chrome handrails so that the Queen and Prince Philip could be seen clearly by all, waving to the crowds.

The vehicle had claret-coloured coachwork and, as is normal for a state vehicle, it had no number plate. It was part of a fleet flown out for the royal couple's six-month Commonwealth tour covering 50,000 miles and taking in Australia, New Zealand, Ceylon, (Sri Lanka), Aden, (Yemen), into Africa and then up to Gibraltar and back to Britain.

In some countries including Australia, local army drivers were specially trained to drive at very slow ceremonial speeds.

Land Rover launched a long-wheelbase version in 1954 and followed up with what was claimed to be the world's first five-door 4x4 station wagon in 1956.

This launch and successive well-publicised international marathon expeditions also triggered a move by many well-funded international competitors to design similarly capable and often larger 4x4 vehicles.

The Queen Mother too had a vehicle customised in the 1960s and with all the royal patronage, the demand for Land Rovers outstripped orders for Rover Cars. It was a golden age for the factory in Solihull.

In 1966 Prince Philip bought JVW 1D, perhaps his all-time favourite Station Wagon and one that he used at events all over the country including Badminton Horse Trials and Windsor. Prince Phillip and Prince Charles delighted in the 'better view' gained by climbing on the bonnet and sitting on the roof.

A little later, a long-wheelbase Land Rover was bought and fitted with a 'gun bus' body which was well used at Sandringham during the shooting season. It is said that Phillip liked it so much that he joked with the Queen that he would rather like it to carry his coffin to his funeral.

Indeed years later, he had a hand in the conversion of that vehicle to turn it into his hearse for his funeral at Windsor in April 2021

Following an accident in January 2019 in his Freelander, Prince Phillip gave up his licence at the age of 97.

Prince Philip's favourite 'JWV' is still owned by the royal family and was used by Prince William and his wife when they were on tour in Scotland last year.

Towards the end of the 1960s, the loyal but now old, Series One, State IV, with its rather low-powered 1,997cc, 52bhp engine, needed replacement but it wasn't until 1971 that planning for a new vehicle began.

Rover's managing director, A B Smith, suggested adapting a Range Rover, though it took two years to agree on the final design with the royal household. State 1, as the vehicle became known, was a standard Range Rover taken off the production line minus its roof, tailgate and side windows.

It was taken to the jig shop at Solihull where the bulkhead behind the driver was moved forward and the fuel tank removed

A 110 WITH AN 'INTERESTING HISTORY'

Loyalty among Land Rover owners runs deep and just as with us mere mortals, the real' Defender that 'died' in 2016 will always be viewed with fond memories.

Memories like those of my grandfather, who was mentioned in dispatches for repeatedly driving his ambulance through the withering gunfire of World War One and refusing to let deep drifts on the snowy Cotswolds stop him from completing his round to outlying farms.

He fitted great chunky Dunlops to his LWB IIA and set off in all weathers – usually with a snow shovel or two in the back to help get him out of trouble.

And as a country boy, having tried many Japanese 4x4s, I would gravitate towards a Defender. At one glorious and brief point, I had three of them.

So when my local dealer advertised a three-year-old, one-owner 110 with very low mileage and an 'interesting history', I went to have a look.

The immaculate Galway Green 110 XS, 2011 seven-seater wasn't cheap, but with various work, recreational and towing needs, this looked like a solid investment, particularly since it turned out to be a royal household vehicle that had been based at Highgrove and Gatcombe and serviced locally by T H White.

I gave it a thorough examination. There were a few surprises, not least getting an interesting view of the tarmac upon lifting a rear carpet. There were several dents on the top of the front wings too. Who, I wondered, had been sitting up there or standing at the horse trials or Siddington Point-to-Point?

The deal was done but what I was really looking for was a five-seater. So I found that those nice people at James French had a conversion kit and could remove the two rear seats, remove the silly, completely impractical carpet, hide the rear seat belts behind the trim and reconstruct the rear load area to reproduce the original Land Rover rubber-covered layout.

Add a full dog guard and there you have the perfect shooting brake (as a joking tilt at its royal past, we did put in a square of red carpet for the labradors to lie on).

So 50,000 very enjoyable miles later, I still have a car that hasn't lost any value and which has travelled all around the country in all weathers; pulled itself and passengers through snowdrifts and many a forest track and mud bath and proved itself an able towing vehicle for vintage tractors and military vehicles.

I have often wondered who had driven the vehicle. I can see from the scratches on the inside of a couple of windows that several richly be-jewelled hands have wiped away some condensation, perhaps on a rainy shoot day.

But when towing my 1942 Willys RAF Jeep around the country, I think of the beaming smile on the face of Queen Elizabeth in 1941 and how her first 4x4 experience ultimately led to her family's long and loyal association with …The 'Best 4x4 By Far'!

'By 1951 Land Rover had won its first Royal Warrant as a supplier of vehicles to the royal family'

Author Neil Huband's former royal household Land Rover Craig Moore

Prince Philip at the Windsor Horse Show alongside his Land Rover Discovery Tim Graham Photo Library via Getty Images

The Queen leads a procession from Horse Guards, along the Mall to Buckingham Palace Sgt Mike Harvey / Crown Copyright

Seventy years after Her Father, King George VI, named the Royal Artillery's Riding Troop as 'The King's Troop Royal Horse Artillery' the Queen inspected the troop on its anniversary parade Cpl Dek Traylor / Crown Copyright

from the rear of the car and repositioned behind the driver. The exhaust system was changed to avoid fumes affecting the occupants and foldaway seats were positioned in the rear compartment.

Half seats provided support for when the royals had been standing during a lengthy parade. There was a lectern positioned over the bulkhead with two umbrellas concealed inside.

The Range Rover was powered by the standard 3,528cc,135 bhp V8 and would have been capable of more than 90mph. Again it had claret-coloured paintwork and carried no number plate.

It finally replaced the Series One in 1974. Fortunately for us motoring enthusiasts, both this unique Range Rover and the famous Series One, now form part of a terrific, not to be missed, display of royal vehicles at The British Motor Museum at

> 'I still have a car that hasn't lost any value and which has travelled all around the country in all weathers'

Gaydon in Warwickshire.

The Range Rover model quickly became popular with the royals, and Charles and Diana were often photographed together with their vehicle.

The Queen was frequently pictured driving her Range Rovers and coinciding with her birthday in 2016, a new Claret-coloured state Ranger Rover with a diesel/ hybrid

power plant was seen for the first time.

Over the years, however, she was often seen driving Series Land Rovers and later Defenders too. Her V8, A444 RYU was particularly popular and then later came the TD5s and latterly the Puma. It has been reported that the Queen has owned as many as 30 Land Rovers throughout her reign.

In recent years several royal household vehicles were loaned to the country homes of members of the royal family by Jaguar Land Rover. I did hear that while the improved heater and less clumsy 'aircon' fittings in the carpeted, leather-seated Puma XS were much appreciated, the bonnet 'hump' raised some eyebrows among hostesses.

Apparently, and unlike the flat bonnet of the much-loved TD5, on the Puma, teacups and wine and beer glasses had an unfortunate tendency to slide off! **CLR**

RECON ROVER

Craig Allen finds out how a former British Army Snatch Land Rover ended up on the frontlines in Ukraine

WORDS **CRAIG ALLEN**
PICTURES **SVITLANA INIAKOZIENE, PAUL PEARCE**

Serhii and his team pose with their newly delivered Snatch Land Rover which is now serving on the frontline

'With its composite armoured body, the
Snatch does at least offer protection from
shell fragments and small arms fire'

AUkrainian national who has been living in Scotland for the past 14 years proved that even though she may be miles from the frontline, she is still able to assist her compatriots in the fight against Russia.

Svitlana Iniakoziene, who is living in Dunfermline with her Lithuanian husband Rimantas and her two children, set about raising money to purchase an armoured vehicle for her brother Serhii Sharko's small reconnaissance team.

Ever since Russia invaded in early 2022, Ukraine has been crying out for armoured vehicles, and while the west has finally responded, the vast scale of the war has meant there is always a need for more essential military equipment. As such, many frontline units are having to make do with unsuitable civilian vehicles.

This is what prompted Serhii to reach out to his sister for help. Serhii ran a small shop in his local village before the war, but like so many of his compatriots, signed up with the military after Russia's invasion. His reconnaissance team were using a beat-up Japanese pickup to ferry them to the front lines. That was back in September 2022, when he and his unit were operating near Soledar, close to Bakhmut: the town that was captured by the Russians in January 2023. His plea didn't go unanswered.

Svitlana initially reached out to the Ukrainian community in the UK for help. Some of her countrymen had originally settled in Britain in the wake of World War Two, so many small towns and villages across the United Kingdom possess some form of Ukrainian community. These clubs and associations have been boosted by the arrival of a fresh wave of refugees following the invasion.

Svitlana and Rimantas were already working with Support the Heroes, a group of volunteers who run charity events to raise money for vital equipment for Ukrainian soldiers. They also received help from a Lithuanian charity which

The Snatch as originally purchased by Paul Pearce, had received significant front-end damage from an IED strike in Iraq and was in generally poor condition

Signs of some of the shrapnel damage incurred during the vehicle's time in Basra

BELOW: 'The Team', Serhii is the tallest and finds the Land Rover driver's seat a tight squeeze

The Snatch in fully refurbished form, a tribute to all the work put in by Paul over the years

Paul had to rebuild the V8 3.5-litre engine, refurbish the brakes and front axle plus fit a new exhaust system among other repairs

assisted with fundraising.

At first, this work concentrated on supplying basic equipment like helmets and body armour, so sourcing an armoured vehicle took things to a whole new level. The couple went door to door leafleting local businesses, and slowly but surely, the funds began to come in. At the same time, they searched for a suitable vehicle that might fall within their limited budget. After doing some research, they eventually settled on a Snatch Land Rover.

The Snatch features armoured protection and has good cross-country ability to cope with the Ukrainian mud. There was only one problem – most of the Land Rovers advertised online were in the £30,000 to £35,000 bracket. This re-focused the fundraising efforts,

and Svitlana came up with the idea of a cultural event using her links to the arts and crafts community. She set about putting things together and approached her local councillor in Dunfermline for help with finding a suitable venue.

The council offered up the old fire station which had been turned into a creative and artistic hub after the fire service moved out. In early November 2022, they held their first event, bringing together both local and Ukrainian craftspeople and artists. It turned out to be a great success, which gave Svitlana the confidence to arrange another event in Edinburgh. She was able to secure the use of St Cuthbert's Church in the capital for an evening of music and entertainment which was well attended.

Despite all of her best efforts, Svitlana was still well short of the budget she would need to buy the Land Rover, and with fighting intensifying in Ukraine, time was pressing. Then, through a stroke of luck, she came across a Snatch being offered on Facebook at an affordable price of £14,500. It was located on the Isle of Portland in

'This represents a real lifesaver to Serhii's small drone unit on their perilous missions at the front'

Dorset, and she contacted the owner Paul Pearce to agree on the sale.

The Snatch was a V8 model, originally issued to the Royal Irish Rangers in Northern Ireland. Paul is a veteran of the same regiment – a factor which first attracted him to the vehicle. It was purchased from a friend of his ten years ago and needed quite a bit of work to put right. The Snatch had spent some time in Iraq with the regiment, serving during the Battle of Basra where it was hit by an IED strike.

As a consequence, there was severe shrapnel damage to the front end and to the armoured windscreens, which had to be replaced. Paul also rebuilt the ➲

Svitlana's determination to help her brother and his comrades was the impetus behind the fundraising events in Dunfermline and Edinburgh

A good turn out including local dignitaries for the music and cultural event held at St Cuthbert's Church in Edinburgh

The Snatch beside one of the unit's civilian vehicles. Before its arrival, Serhii and his team had to rely on an old Japanese pickup

The capacious internal load area of the Snatch is ideal for the team and all its gear, they would just like a few gun ports

3.5lt V8 engine, fitted a new clutch, and refurbished the brakes – replacing all the pipes for stainless steel.

Due to the blast damage, the front axle also had to be rebuilt and a new stainless steel exhaust was fitted. Paul restored the rest of the vehicle and displayed it on the show circuit, as well as attending various fundraising events for the Royal British Legion. Before handing it over, he generously fitted a complete set of new tyres, for which Svitlana was very grateful.

With the Snatch finally purchased and prepared, the next problem was how to get the vehicle to Serhii and his unit in eastern Ukraine. Thankfully, a friend stepped in to offer his services to ferry the vehicle across Europe.

Antanas Vytekas was another ex-patriot Ukrainian who was working in Germany as a lorry driver. Antanas flew to the UK to pick up the Land Rover, driving it to Dover for the crossing to Dunkirk. His route then took him through France, Belgium and the Netherlands, before arriving at his home in Bremerhaven, Germany.

After a few days' rest, he continued through Poland to reach the border with Ukraine. All through the road journey, the Land Rover stirred up interest with people wanting to photograph it at fuel and rest stops. Once over the border, he still had a long drive through western Ukraine to reach the small village of Trebukhiv, just outside of Kyiv, where the handover took place.

Here he met up with Serhii, and members of the family, for an emotional welcome after the long trek across Europe. Antanas then flew back to Germany while Serhii re-joined

'So far the vehicle has proved very reliable, with the only repair needed being a replacement oil sensor'

his unit with the prized Land Rover. The Snatch was quickly put to work in support of Ukrainian forces fighting in Eastern Ukraine.

The Snatch Land Rover has something of a chequered history, as the vehicle proved fatally vulnerable to roadside bombs during operations in Iraq. However, it should be remembered that the US Humvee often suffered a similar fate during the insurgency following the 2003 invasion.

The simple fact is, that neither of these vehicles was designed to withstand blasts from powerful IEDs. The Snatch was originally intended as a lightly armoured patrol vehicle for use in Northern Ireland.

I remember these Land Rovers from a tour of the province in the early 1990s, and they were excellent for use in low-threat environments. We didn't risk taking them into the hard areas of West Belfast, where heavier armoured APV Land Rovers were employed. It might therefore seem ironic that this example has found a place in the middle of a full-blown war zone. That is until you consider that Serhii and his comrades were previously using a civilian pickup to reach the front lines.

With its composite armoured body, the Snatch does at least offer protection from shell fragments and small arms fire – thus making it far superior to the pickup previously used by the team.

This represents a real lifesaver to Serhii's small drone unit on their perilous missions at the front. Once operating they don't loiter in an area for more than 40-45 minutes at a time, before rapidly moving location. Staying in one place for too long risks being spotted by Russian drones or forward observers, and thus drawing mortar and artillery fire.

Serhii has since told Classic Land Rover that apart from the useful protection it offers, the Snatch has great cross-country ability, as the group often has to operate off-road. There is also plenty of room in the back for the team and all its equipment.

The few disadvantages he noted were the cramped driver's position, especially for tall people such as himself. The lack of

Serhii flashes a victory sign with his young daughter when the Land Rover arrives after its long trek across Europe

gun ports was another feature he noted as a disadvantage. British practice was to have a couple of soldiers manning the roof hatch as 'top cover', although this did leave them exposed to enemy fire.

Despite the powerful V8 engine, Serhii has also said they found the maximum speed is quite low. The latter is undoubtedly a feature of the Snatch's weight and low gearing, and Antanas did note on the delivery journey that he couldn't get it over 70mph. As many of us know, this is quite fast for a Defender, and it's more than likely a case of the crew being unfamiliar with the vehicle.

So far it has proved very reliable, with the only repair needed being a replacement oil sensor. The team has made a couple of modifications, such as removing the large antenna boxes and fitting a Webasto heater into the back. Overall, they have been impressed with the excellent condition of the vehicle, doubtless due to the work put in by Paul during his ownership.

This veteran Land Rover is now doing its duty on the frontline, and its arrival made Serhii and his team the envy of their regiment. This is all down to the fantastic efforts of Svitlana, Rimantas and all those who helped raise the necessary funds. This is an uplifting tale and goes to show what's possible at the individual level given enough determination and support. 'Slava Ukraini'. **CLR**

A Land Rover press image of the Range Rover when launched in 1970

THE LAUNCH OF A
LEGEND

Author **Eric Dymock** was at the 1970
launch of the Range Rover and recalls the
hype around the vehicle

WORDS AND PICTURES **ERIC DYMOCK / LAND ROVER**

T he Range Rover press launch came the week before the Belgian Grand Prix. June 1970 was also Le Mans and the Dutch Grand Prix, and I was covering motor racing for The Guardian.

I was freelance, so also did car launches, comments, and road tests for the paper's regular motoring correspondent. He was away that week so passed on an invitation to Meudon Hotel, Falmouth for the Range Rover launch.

Since 1948, Land Rovers had been agricultural or military. Now, on the brink of being something else, their publicists were unsettled. Rovers, "One of Britain's Fine Cars" were always understated, quiet, confident, cars that knew where they were going. Land Rovers were a side-line until post-war steel allocations improved so, in the 1960s when they took on a life of their own, it came as a surprise. A success on quiet farms, deserts, jungles, swamps and world trouble spots, Land Rovers spoke for themselves.

So, to Fleet Street motoring correspondents on the 10.10 from Paddington to Penzance, Range Rover's press office's material came

'Nothing this big and heavy had ever sustained speed with such confidence'

with the gravitas of a proclamation from the Post Office. "Not for publication until Wednesday, 17th June, 1970. A revolutionary new model combining the luxury and comfort of the world-famous Rover saloon car range, the acceleration and handling characteristics of many high-performance cars, the stylish body of an estate car, and the ruggedness, durability, and cross-country versatility of the renowned Land-Rover, is announced by the Rover Company."

True, although scarcely succinct. They weren't even sure what to call it. "Range Rover" was inspired. Road Rovers had been tried in 1953 but the prototypes had been too heavy.

The press office thought it might be an "estate car" or "Station Wagon" but couldn't make up its mind about capitals. It was sure

about a "highly competitive contender for the valuable and fast-growing four-wheel-drive 'leisure' market", whatever that was.

They were on firm ground with a trendy "car for all reasons" trailing Robert Bolt's screenplay A Man for All Seasons, still doing cinema rounds. That gave it a familiar ring. Yet convincing the great and good of Fleet Street would take more than Post Office English and a posh hotel in Mawnan Smith.

I always felt safer on press test drives to team up with somebody I knew. John Blunsden, my motor racing counterpart at The Times, was on the train.

We trusted one another's driving and sat in First Class behind Inter-City Great Western D800 diesels learning, alas, sad news. Bruce McLaren, whom we knew and liked, had died the previous day at Goodwood testing a Can-Am car.

 Journalists at the 1970 launch soon realised the Range Rover offered the best combination on and off-road, with high clearance and astonishing agility

We were bussed into Meudon Hotel's 8.5 acres of subtropical gardens, giant rhubarb plants leading to Bream Cove and a waiting line of Range Rovers.

Cornwall was sunlit and calm. Land's End trial hills such as Beggars Roost beckoned as a test route. Both of us had tested the Rover 2000 and knew the preoccupations of Charles Spencer King (1925-2010), one of the dynasty that ran Rover.

Reserved, gifted, empirical engineer, 'Spen' King, a wartime apprentice at Rolls-Royce, had made space in the 2000 for a gas turbine. It never got one, but its appliqué body panels on a stiff frame provided exemplary ride and handling and he adapted them for the crisp, well-proportioned newcomer.

King's genius was never appreciated at British Leyland. Neither was that of another from the dynasty, William Martin-Hurst, who had invented a market research department under economist Graham Bannock.

It was telling him Land Rover was likely to expand only at the leisure, high-priced end of the market. Sales to the military and police were fine, but a generation of private buyers towing boats, caravans and horseboxes no longer liked harshly sprung Land Rovers.

A visit to America in 1965 convinced Bannock that sports-utility vehicles (SUVs) such as the Jeep Wagoneer, International

The launch was held in Cornwall with beautiful backdrops adding to the overall experience

The Range Rover was both cleverly styled and cleverly named

Range Rovers were comfortable, roomy, and highly practical

Harvester Scout and Ford Bronco were laying more sophisticated wheel tracks.

Road Rover dreams of the 1950s, according to Bannock, were worth reviving. King started work in 1966 as the Harold Wilson government sped things up.

Purchase tax was hitting car sales. Military withdrawal east of Suez, a financial crisis and devaluation affected defence spending.

Bannock was right and some sort of SUV, with long-travel, low-rate coil springing such as King had invented for the Rover 2000,

was best. A trial drive of a 2000 in a bumpy field convinced King, and there was already a V8 Land Rover to provide an engine.

Blunsden and I drove cheerfully around a prescribed route past Goonhilly Down. In those days car-makers provided chase vehicles in case a journalist got lost, strayed off to a pub (it wasn't unknown) or crashed (that wasn't unknown either) or their car failed.

After a short time, we concluded that here, at last, was something new. It was

the best combination on and off-road, with high clearance and astonishing agility, we had ever driven.

Range Rovers were comfortable, roomy, and fast. You could drive into a field and, provided it was not deeply ploughed, need scarcely slacken speed. Bumps disappeared up the marshmallow springs.

Land Rover always thought a harsh ride a good thing; it slowed drivers up, so they didn't tend to break axles or leaf springs. King was convinced that supple long-travel suspension not only provided an even ride but also better articulation. Range Rovers always kept their wheels in contact with the ground. Any that lost touch lost drive.

I took pictures of Blunsden demonstrating it. On wet rocks, potholes 2ft deep from crest to crest, wet sand, loose boulders, clay and combinations up gradients of nearly 1:1.

He crawled the car out of the craters. If one set of wheels lost grip, he operated a button locking up all four to prevent drive leaking away to one hanging in mid-air. Range Rovers had a stirring road performance, swift acceleration and most of the tranquillity expected of a Rover.

The transfer gears whined. There were Rover engineers on the launch who told us they would eliminate that, but they never did.

The Michelin X M+S tubed radial tyres howled a bit at 95mph but, like the rest of the vehicle, were a revelation. Nothing this big and heavy had ever sustained speed with such confidence yet these Michelins were still able to cope with flints and sharp rocks.

At £2 short of £2,000 the new Range Rover was a bargain. Aimed at the prosperous market Bannock identified for countryside pursuits, going on safari in comfort or simply looking squirearchical, it was cleverly styled and cleverly named.

Bigger and longer than regular Land Rovers, although not quite as tall, you could see over traffic – a privilege not afforded to lower-order saloon drivers.

The interior was well laid out. They had planned it to be as luxurious as Rover cars, but the walnut veneer and carpets had to wait. Practicality took precedence and in a rare display of publicity skill, Rover claimed the thick plastic floor covering had been designed from the start to be washed down with a hose.

Gentleman farmers hadn't wanted the trappings of a saloon, Rover told us. They were getting a car to drive in gumboots or city slip-ons that somehow felt best in brogues.

The truth was that interior design planning had gone badly. The hose-down story was a cover-up. We were impressed at the self-contained seats so firmly fixed they had their own integral seatbelts.

Why, we wondered, had safety legend Volvo not thought of that? What we didn't know was that these had taken so long to develop they nearly held up the entire launch.

As it was, Rover's press kit warned sternly: "Initial supplies of this vehicle will be restricted to the UK market. Further details of its international debut will be announced in a short time.

"To avoid disappointment by the general public it is essential that when reporting about this vehicle on the announcement day, it is made absolutely clear that even supplies to the home market will not start until September 1st. This delay will enable…"

We dutifully reported to the general public. What a success the Range Rover was. King's design work and Martin-Hurst's discovery of a Buick V8 facing scrappage had been inspirational. **CLR**

'They had planned it to be as luxurious as Rover cars, but the walnut veneer and carpets had to wait'

Whether used for work, going on safari or other leisure pursuits, the Range Rover did all that was asked of it

I sat on the train from London to Halifax in West Yorkshire with a one-way ticket, seemingly a giveaway of my intention. On arrival in the town, I met Olli, the owner of a 1969 Land Rover Series IIA diesel that I'd made the trip north for. Olli had rescued it from a barn on a farm in Yorkshire two months earlier where it had once previously been used as a run-around.

It was love at first sight and I asked Olli if he thought I could safely drive it back to London. "If you are willing to do 200 miles at a maximum speed of 40mph, I'm certain you'll make it," came the reply. Eight hours later, with a few stops on the way, I was back in London, the proud owner of a piece of British motoring history.

The next morning, once my excitement had settled down, I started the vehicle to show my young children our new toy but was met with an uninvited cloud of black smoke. I naively told myself that everything would be alright once the engine warmed up a bit. But I was wrong.

'Like most Land Rover owners, I like to get my hands dirty and having an electric Land Rover doesn't change this'

After consulting Google, YouTube and a local Land Rover specialist I made a few attempts to clean its 'lungs' but alas, nothing worked, and I had to live with my smoky Land Rover until I could come up with a solution.

I'd wait until there were no pedestrians around before starting up, wave apologetically to every cyclist I passed and was genuinely embarrassed to be contributing towards pollution in the health-conscious city of London.

This embarrassment was made worse because I work in the air quality and air pollution field. In 2018 I stood in front of the nation on Dragons' Den to pitch my company, Brizi, which is on a mission to protect babies from air pollution, so it didn't feel right.

Morally I thought, I could never drive a Land Rover again! And so there it stood for months, unused apart from a few trips out of town, while I investigated my options.

I soon came across information about converting classic cars to electric power. This was not something I had ever considered or even heard of, but it certainly got me interested in finding out more.

LONDON CALLING

Embarrassed by the smoke his 1969 Series IIA was giving off, **Yosi Romano** decided to go electric

WORDS **YOSI ROMANO**
PICTURES **SHIRA KLASMER PHOTOGRAPHY**

Converting to electric power has made the Series IIA much easier to live with in London

Yosi's daughters Alma, 9, and Livya, 5, are big fans of 'Landy'

Canvas door pouches allow for extra storage

A good spot for some tailgate tea or coffee

'The Land Rover charges at 6.6kw, which is the speed that most electric cars charge'

After gathering a couple of quotes for the work to be done, I quickly realised just how new the industry is. Most companies wanted to fully restore my Land Rover, and then electrify it and came back with prices more than £100,000, not to mention a three-year waiting list. The only way I'd be able to afford that was by winning the lottery.

However, determined not to give up, I continued my search and eventually came across Electric Car Converts, a start-up in Sussex trying to make electric vehicle conversions affordable, supposedly for people like me.

I contacted the owner, Barnaby, who told me that they don't build conversions with crazy horsepower and they don't build with hundreds of miles of range, but they do electrify Land Rovers for cheaper than buying a new 'budget' electric city car. This sounded perfect.

Delighted that I now had a solution, I told my family of my plans one dinnertime but could immediately tell by the look on my eldest daughter, Alma's, face that she was not impressed. Her main worry was that 'Landy' (that's the name she's given it) would lose its character.

Alma wanted to keep the rattle and the noise and agreed to my plan only after I again explained that we couldn't use the vehicle in town with the amount of black smoke it spewed. I made a promise that I would preserve the rest of Landy's character by never painting it, even the heavily patinaed rear tub, caused by hay bales in its previous life.

So, back to Barnaby, I went. Due to his

The interior is really neat

The current range on the vehicle is 70 miles, but that could be increased if needed

speciality in Land Rovers, he explained that it was important to start with a good vehicle with good brakes, suspension and a solid chassis, as it wasn't worth converting a "rust bucket like so many of them are". So, he recommended I talk to a restorer before embarking on the project. It made sense as I didn't want to put 120hp of battery-powered goodness into a car that couldn't stop.

To get Landy's EV conversion ready, I approached Joel from RestoRovers, who changed the leaf springs to a set of softer ones, made a tiny repair and rust- treated the chassis and checked everything was in good order. Four new tyres later I pootled down into the Sussex countryside to drop my pride and joy off with Electric Car Converts.

Landy was electrified to the following specifications:

RANGE AND BATTERIES

I opted for the short-range option, which was five Tesla Module S batteries (26.5kWh) mounted under the bonnet, giving me around 70 miles of range. People often say to me 70 miles is nowhere near enough but when you think about it, how often do you drive more than 70 miles in a day? I do about 70 miles in a week around London. Importantly, when I am ready to extend the range I can take it back to have another battery pack installed.

MOTOR

An American 'Hyper9' electric motor was installed, which produces 120hp and 235Nm of torque, more than double what my 2,286cc diesel engine had put out before. This allows me to accelerate

quickly and keep up with modern-day London traffic, which improves driveability. The motor is coupled to the original gearbox through a series of complicated adapter plates (machined within a 1,000th of an inch), which means the original flywheel and clutch are used. I spend most of my time in third gear around town (I never need first or second due to the huge torque), changing into fourth when I go onto any faster road. When I go off-road, I can still engage my original four-wheel drive system and low-ratio box.

CHARGING

The Land Rover charges at 6.6kw, which is the speed that most electric cars charge. It can be charged at any EV charging station, be it outside the supermarket, ⟳

at a lamppost or the motorway services, allowing a full 0-100% charge in four hours. However, most of the time I plug it in on a normal three-pin plug outside my house, which tops the charge up each night ready for another day of carting my kids around.

OTHER

Due to being significantly lighter under the bonnet (200kg worth of batteries and motor instead of a 350kg engine plus fuel, plus radiator etc), Landy is much easier to steer without any power steering, making life a bit easier during a tight London parallel park. It has also got a high voltage heater installed, which means instant heat in the mornings (think a hairdryer on steroids). This is mounted in the original heater box, meaning the original ducting and heater controls are used.

LIVING IN LONDON

I've since found that driving an electric car in London comes with many benefits, both financially and environmentally. I now produce zero grams of CO_2 per mile, compared to 390 grams previously and my cost per mile is down from 39p to just 9p. I no longer pay a surcharge for diesel and get a huge discount as an electric vehicle on my residential parking permit, plus I can drive into the city centre without paying the congestion charge.

'I soon came across information about converting classic cars to electric power'

And if I did pay road tax, I would now be tax-exempt. I have even ended up convincing parking apps that my 1969 Land Rover is an electric vehicle, which itself was quite a process, but I now get the discount I deserve.

Along with most Land Rover owners, I like to get my hands dirty and having an electric Land Rover doesn't change this. I still spend hours tinkering, whether that be putting my spare wheel on the bonnet, touching up the odd rust bubble, fixing the speedometer cable or greasing the driveshaft. Importantly, Alma is happy because it's still an old Land Rover and still behaves like one.

When people who know a thing or two about Land Rovers see me before they hear me, the surprise and disbelief are very amusing. I'm constantly approached in car parks where I'm asked about the process and whether I'm happy with my decision to convert. I can honestly say that I'm very pleased to drive a car that I genuinely love without contributing to London's smog. **CLR**

Crossing Westminster Bridge. Yosi's no longer worried about contributing towards pollution

SAFARI EQUIPPERS & SEAT COVER SPECIALISTS

Wheel Covers

Seat Covers

Roll-up Games

Short Safari Duffel

Rift Valley

Dashboard Cover & Canvas Hat

Steffi Halm 07780335521
steffi@melvillandmoon.com

MELVILLANDMOON.CO.UK

AUTOELECTRICAL COMPONENTS
www.simtekuk.co.uk

SIMTEK (UK)™ stocks many connectors including those used in Land Rovers, Fords and BMWs - avilable as kits, in bulk supply and/or with wire tails fitted to perfectly suit your application. Feel free to visit our website, call us or email for help!

All SIMTEK (UK)™ products are designed and made in the UK to ensure the quality you need and the service you deserve.

Buy better – buy British!

Simtek (UK)™'s DASHDAPTER™ integrates while you innovate! Our BodyLogic™ range has been integrating Vehicle Electrics and Electronics for over two decades. Great for...
- CONVERSIONS
- CUSTOMISATIONS
- RESTORATIONS

We have three models of increasing capability - so what's your next project?

For more details feel free to contact us!

AUTOELECTRONIC CONTROLS

telephone: 01706 854857   email: sales@simtekuk.co.uk   www.bodylogicuk.com

Nick Dimbleby joins a convoy of Land Rovers driving from Melbourne to Cooma for the 75th Anniversary celebrations

WORDS AND PICTURES **NICK DIMBLEBY**

Having decided to travel halfway around the world to go to the Cooma Land Rover show, the last 500 miles from Melbourne to Cooma was the bit I was most looking forward to.

The flight via Hong Kong had taken 24 hours and had been at an average speed of 500mph, whereas the drive across Victoria's High Country was to be at a more sedately average of 5mph. We could have taken the tarmac road of course, but where's the fun in that? Given the choice of driving for hours on the tarmac or meandering our way through the bush, the more relaxed route off-road was by far the best choice.

The assortment of vehicles in our mini convoy was good. There were two pre-1500 1948 80ins, as well as a beautifully patinated 1950 80in, a 1953 Australian CKD 80in, a 1956 107in pick-up and a 1958 107in Station Wagon. Supporting these old timers was a 2013 Defender 90 Station Wagon, a much-modified 2015 Defender 130 Ute and a 2015 Discovery 4: a perfect set of vehicles to drive 500 miles predominantly off-road from the east of Melbourne to Cooma.

One of the 1948 80ins proudly wore a grille badge from the first Cooma Land Rover 40th Anniversary event held in 1988, and since 1993 that vehicle has been on permanent display in a museum. How cool was it to be driving the old Land Rover back to Cooma off-road after three decades parked up indoors?

If you think the vehicles were varied,

'That night there was a full moon, which illuminated the campsite'

then you should have seen the drivers. Our team was a mix of Australian, British and US enthusiasts, most of whom were Series One experts. You couldn't wish for a better collection of mechanics and Series One gurus: we had Mike Bishop from Land Rover Classic, Alex Massey from CKD Shop, Ike Goss and Linus Tremaine from Pangolin 4x4, Jackson Senes from Artefact Motor Co and the independent Series Land Rover restorer Brett Gottdener from the US. With that huge bank of knowledge, any conceivable issue that we might have could be easily dealt with, and to back it all up, every one of these folks brought along a choice set of spares that proved useful during the trip.

Australian Land Rover collector Doriano del Monaco drove his own 1948 80in (the former museum piece I mentioned earlier), and he was also generous enough to lend Linus and his partner Maddi, Jackson and Brett the two long-wheelbase Series Ones from his collection. Rob Leseberg (formerly of Melbourne's ULR dealership) drove his Discovery 4 in support, while Mike Bishop drove the second 1948 80in which he's owned since the 1990s. Mike also lent Ike and his partner Jenna his 1953 80in known as JDO. The other 80 belongs to fellow Aussie Alex Massey, and he drove it for most of the trip.

Finally, in the two support Defenders was UK Camel Trophy winner and all-round expedition and travel expert Bob Ives, along with his son Dan driving the Defender 130 load hauler (also owned by Alex). As I was generally having to scout ahead to try and take photos as the convoy motored past, I drove Mike's 2.2lt Puma 90 that lives with his family in Australia. What a team!

After flying into Australia and completing the necessary pre-trip checks, we all met at Doriano's house in the countryside east of Melbourne. The plan was to camp out in tents or swags every night, with food cooked on a (safely managed) open fire, so a lot of pre-trip preparation and shopping had already been done by the time most of us arrived.

As only a few of the team live in Australia (Alex and Mike are Aussies living in the UK), the majority of the vehicles had been in storage for a while, so they needed to be dusted off and prepared for the trip. Ike, Jenna, Linus and Maddi helped get Mike's two vehicles ready, and Alex drove his 130 and 80in down from Queensland – a mere 1,000 miles – just to get started. Australia's a big place.

After setting off, our first stop was the fuel station in nearby Emerald, where bonnets were lifted for the first time to do a bit of pre-trail maintenance. After filling up, it became apparent that the fuel tank on Mike's 1953 80in had a slight leak, which meant that we had to make a detour to visit his Uncle Ken's farm, where – remarkably – Mike knew he had a spare fuel tank tucked away. This tank had been salvaged from an old Series One that Mike had broken for spares years ago, and it was ceremoniously handed over to Ike later that day.

Another nice little stop en route was the Noojee Trestle Bridge, a spectacular 21m-tall wooden structure dating from 1919. It served the Noojee to Warragul railway

Maddi and Linus in Doriano's wonderfully original 1956 107 pick-up

Mike Bishop and Bob Ives consult the map

Wonderful wing-top catering by Jenna Fribley

until the late 1950s, and during this time it partially burnt down twice. It fell into disrepair in the 1980s but was completely restored in the late 1990s – a bit like some of the Land Rovers on the trip.

From Noojee, the final destination for the day was the Brunton Bridge Camping Area on the edge of the Baw Baw National Park, south of the old-world village of Walhalla. The track to Brunton's Bridge saw the first technical off-roading, with a climb up into the hills along some steep and undulating gravel tracks.

The following morning, the dampness in the air combined with the cold ground temperature shrouded part of the hills in mist, which offered a great opportunity for some moody photos in the woods. Perfect, until JDO decided to stop working. Ike and Jackson tried hard to get it to run nicely (they'd already changed the leads and points before leaving), but it was Mike who saved the day by whipping out a spare rotor arm that he happened to have about his person and replacing it in the distributor. Problem solved.

Our next test was the relatively shallow ford by Brunton's Bridge. Despite some concern about the ability of Series Ones to wade through water, all the vehicles made it through successfully and we headed along the meandering track to the edge of the hills near Cowwarr. Here, the hills dropped down onto an open plain, the trees thinning out to reveal miles and miles of flatland to the east.

We turned our backs to the flatlands though, heading north towards the hills and at Licola we filled up at the old-fashioned fuel pumps outside the town's general store. With the old Land Rovers parked up outside, it looked like a scene that could have been from any time over the past 70 years; except, that is, for the satellite dish on the side of the building.

From Licola we entered the start of the Victoria High Country proper, climbing gently at first, then steeper until we crossed the ridgeline at Bastards Neck and dropped down 1,000m along the Zeka Spur track to the Wonnangatta Homestead

Early morning mist at the Taylor's Crossing campsite

Flat. Arriving here at sunset allowed us to enjoy a bit of a sort-out and a nice meal around the campfire. After a visit to the old cemetery nearby, one of our number told us about the 'Button Man', an individual so named because of his coat buttons fashioned from bone.

The Button Man is a mysterious bushman, who lives in the wilds of the Wonnangatta Valley, living off the land, hunting with a traditional spear and supposedly turning up at travellers' campsites once it gets dark. Experienced bush travellers have said that he appears out of nowhere, asks visitors why they are there, and then disappears as stealthily as he arrived. He is said to have "a 1,000m stare that makes the hairs on the back of your neck stand up," and is known to make rock pyramids or wood structures in random places. With reports of people disappearing in the bush without explanation, such stories left a chill down the spine.

After a thankfully uneventful night, Ike and Alex carried out some running repairs to their vehicles in the morning. Ike replaced JDO's fuel tank with the salvaged one that didn't leak, while Alex made a temporary repair to his leaking '49 radiator by using some Radweld. After a couple of hours of work, both leaks were fixed, while Jenna and others prepared a fantastic breakfast of bacon and egg. A great start to the day.

Heading southeast down the Hummfray River Track, we encountered some of the trickiest driving on the route so far. Deeply rutted mud required careful route selection, while deep water crossings tested the Series Ones to the limit. The main issue with wading a Series One is the rotating fan that picks up water and sprays it all over the electrics, causing the vehicle to stall and come to a halt in the middle of the water. One way around this is to remove the fan belt, and this worked a treat. Judicious use of WD40 was also useful.

On one particularly rutted section, Bob Ives managed to beach the heavily loaded Defender 130, requiring a tow from Jenna in the '53 80in JDO. It was impressive seeing the little Land Rover extract the Defender from the mire, although the

tables were turned at the next deep water section when Bob towed Jenna through to prevent the engine from becoming drowned. What goes around comes around.

At the start of the Hart Spur Track, we turned south and headed up into the Cynthia Range on a track which climbed and climbed for what seemed forever. The total elevation change was 'only' 800m, but because it went straight up rather than using switchbacks, the gradient was steep and long: it felt serious.

The little Series Ones had to work hard, with the relatively heavy 107 Station Wagon chugging away. There were a few hairy moments when vehicles ran out of puff in higher gears, but everyone made it over the hills without incident, ending up in the town ➲

On the trail in Doriano del Monaco's beautiful 1948 80in. Up until a few months ago, this vehicle had spent 30 years in a museum – now it's living its best life

of Dargo where we stayed the night in the historic Dargo Hotel (established in 1898).

By this stage in the trip, Doriano's 1948 80in - the former museum piece - was starting to misbehave. It was smoking badly and seemed to be consuming water at an alarming pace. On the first tarmac section leaving Dargo, Doriano had to pull over several times to fill the radiator, leading him to say: 'I'm out,' after the third stop. Of course, abandoning the vehicle and having it recovered was simply not an option, so when half the convoy was halted at a road closure for roadworks on the Dargo High Plains Road, the decision was made to replace the water pump there and then with a secondhand spare that Ike 'just happened' to have with him.

Watching such a knowledgeable collection of Series One experts coming together to replace the water pump in the middle of a forest was a real pleasure.

Early evening light on the Zeka Spur track

Series Ones don't like water, but a little WD40 goes a long way.

'The 'Snowy Hydro' is one of the reasons why Land Rovers are so popular in Australia'

It looked like a surgical procedure, with removed parts placed on a tarp and everything carried out calmly and methodically. When it became apparent that there wasn't a gasket for the pump in the spares kit, Jackson got out his pencil and knife and cut one out from the cardboard from a San Pellegrino water box. We resisted the temptation to fill the radiator with San Pellegrino too.

By this point, the fumes from the mildly poorly Land Rover were giving Doriano a hard time, so for the rest of the trip, he removed the soft top, door tops and tilt frame, even going so far as lowering the windscreen for the full 'wind in the hair' effect. Series Ones really do look their coolest when they're fully stripped like this. With the water pump replaced, Doriano was off again, albeit with the occasional puff of blue smoke from the exhaust.

Passing through the ski resort of Mount Hotham (elevation 1,857m), our little convoy felt on top of the world, with panoramic views every way you looked. Even though the sun was out, the altitude made things feel decidedly chilly, so we were glad to descend back down through Omeo to a riverside campsite at Taylors Crossing. There was a nice campground on the

Mike Bishop's 1948 and Alex Massey's 1950 pause by the Noojee Trestle Bridge

A fabulous convoy of Series Ones makes its way across the Wonnangata Homestead Flat

closest side of the river, but on the other side there was an even nicer place to pitch the tents, but the river looked deep. It took Doriano about 30 seconds to decide that he was going to drive across, and the plucky 75-year-old (the vehicle) made it through unbowed. We were all quick to follow.

That night there was a full moon, which illuminated the campsite through the tall trees on the other side of the river. Some of the group decided to drive up a narrow track to look at a semi-derelict hut at the top of the hill, but on their way back, their route was blocked by mysterious cairns and structures made from sticks that weren't there on the way up. Was it the Button Man?

After a third mysterious structure in the road, people were starting to become concerned. And then it happened. A hooded figure leapt out of the darkness with a roar, prompting everyone to jump about a foot in the air. Fortunately though, our 'Button Man' turned out to be no more sinister than Doriano in a poncho, so we headed back to the campfire for a much-needed drink.

The last couple of days of the trip saw us driving due east across the final part of Victoria's High Country and into New South Wales at Tom Groggin Campsite. The Kosciuszko National Park provided the last panoramic views before we dropped into the town of Jindabyne, situated next to the enormous Jindabyne Reservoir – part of the Snowy Mountain Hydro-Electric scheme that was started back in 1949.

The 'Snowy Hydro' is one of the reasons why Land Rovers are so popular in Australia. Once construction began in

early 1949, a reliable and capable means of getting around the various sites in the rugged and, er, snowy, Snowy Mountains was required, and with the Land Rover having been launched a few months before the start of works, the little 4x4 was seen as tailor-made for the project. Within a year, the Snowy Hydro scheme was one of the largest single non-military users of Land Rovers worldwide and the rest is history.

This historic connection with Snowy Hydro also explains why the nearby town of Cooma has been the home of Australian Land Rover events since the

40th anniversary in 1988. The Snowy Hydro scheme is still very active, with the latest phase - Snowy Hydro 2.0 - starting in 2019. Its promise of sustainable, green energy is totally of the moment, but nowadays things are rather different on the vehicle fleet. Today, Snowy Hydro uses Toyota Hi-Lux pick-ups and Subaru 4WD cars, Land Rovers being consigned to the history books.

Times change and the world moves on, but one thing's for sure, it was a lot of fun taking a bunch of 70-year-old Land Rovers across a landscape that has changed little over the past few centuries. Long may it be possible to do so – roll on 2028. **CLR**

The team pauses for a photo before heading out into Victoria's High Country

Paolo Turinetti carried out a sensitive rebuild to restore the dignity of this iconic Ninety

The Ninety had been abandoned and neglected for some years before Paolo bought it

The Warn winch would need a complete refurb

The 2.5 NA diesel engine hadn't been turned over in years

TECHNICAL DATA

Land Rover Ninety Station Wagon:
Italian 2 Team, Borneo Camel Trophy 1985

Chassis: SALLDVBC8AA228184

Engine: 12J, diesel 2.5 N/A

Built: 18/01/1985

Dispatched: 18/01/1985 to Vehicle
Engineering, Drayton Road

Original UK plate: B 633 COG

Indonesian plate for event: KT 1328 XX

Trophy Truck

Collector Paolo Turinetti's perseverance
paid off when he finally had the opportunity
to acquire this Camel Trophy Ninety

EDITED BY **ROS WOODHAM**   ORIGINAL TEXT **PAOLO TURINETTI**
PICTURES **PAOLO TURINETTI**

Eight years ago Italian Land Rover enthusiast Paolo Turinetti became the owner of the Japanese team's Camel Trophy Discovery which took part in the Mongolia event in 1997.

Having already joined the official Camel Trophy Club his interest in the legendary saga widened and he began to take part in specialist events all over Europe with his treasured Disco.

Paolo is no stranger to classic Land Rovers having owned seven Series Ones, four Series IIs and two Series IIIs so his new-found interest in Camel Trophy seemed like a natural progression.

Before long he became the administrator of the Camel Trophy Italia Facebook page along with friend and journalist Francesco Fatichenti whose 4x4 magazine Paolo contributes to regularly.

It was Francesco who discovered the possibility that a 1985 Borneo Camel Trophy Ninety could be somewhere in the country. He had the name of the alleged owner who was residing around central Italy.

Curious, Paolo began his research on the internet, matching the name with an archaeologist working in Rome, and then digging up a possible email address. With a stab in the dark, Paolo contacted him and to his delight, it was indeed the owner of the elusive Ninety.

An extensive email exchange ensued

Paolo enlisted the help of good friend Roberto to rescue the sad-looking Ninety

yielding more information about the vehicle. It had been from one of the two Italian teams, driven by Roberto Ive and Beppe Gualini.

The owner also divulged that, because of the high taxes on diesel 4x4s in Italy during the mid-nineties, he had removed some major fittings and accessories such as the roll cage and winch as well as replaced the rear side windows with solid panels which put it into a lower tax class. Thankfully he had safely stored the parts in a barn so that they could be refitted at a later date.

The two had developed a good rapport until, perhaps overstepping the mark, Paolo asked if he would consider selling the car. He never received a reply.

Undeterred, Paolo continued sending him greetings for Christmas, Easter, and new year, for three years until, eventually, in August 2021 he received the reply he had been hoping for. Something in the mind or life of the owner had changed and the possibility of Paolo owning the Ninety was finally becoming a reality.

However, the gem that Paolo had been dreaming of had been lying, abandoned and exposed to the elements for almost seven years. It was in such bad condition that the owner repeatedly questioned Paolo's desire for the truck.

Paolo was adamant, of course, but even so, he and his "very understanding wife", drove the 700km to Viterbo, mid-Italy, to see it before agreeing to the sale.

Paolo is no stranger to extensive restorations, such as with HUE 222 (featured in CLR issue 46) – the only 'HUE'-plated Series One known to be in existence other than the original pre-production HUE 166 – so he was not put off by the Ninety's apparent deterioration that he witnessed on arrival. Sale agreed.

Arrangements were made with his friend Roberto to collect the truck two weeks later using his Defender 110 Tdi as the tow vehicle. The two-day round-trip covered 1,500km and took in some pleasant stops such as Lido de Tarquinia on the west coast and the Tuscan city of Arezzo.

The Ninety was then delivered into the care of another friend whose job it was to run a full service and restart the engine which hadn't turned over in some years. In just a few days it was alive again, with a working clutch and brakes, ready to drive to Paolo's lock-up.

Paolo tasked himself with the cleaning – an arduous assignment given the years of

Rear windows re-installed since being removed to comply with commercial vehicle tax status

Indonesian registration plates recreated by Daniel Prasetio from Jakarta

Steel rims shot blasted and repainted

Original cloth seats were expertly repaired and replaced by a local seamstress

Painstaking work to remove and restore the original bolt-on accessories

Due to extreme flooding during the Borneo Camel Trophy event, a helicopter had to be used to lift vehicles to safety

CAMEL TROPHY 1985:
BORNEO

Winners: Heinz Kallin & Bernd Strohdach (West Germany)
Team Spirit: Carlos Probst & Tito Rosenberg (Brazil)
Trucks: Land Rover Ninety (competitors), Land Rover One Ten (support)

Borneo was host to three Camel Trophies (including one on the Malaysian side of the island). In this particular year, 16 teams from eight countries were selected from around half a million applications, with Japan, Brazil, and the Canary Islands making their first appearances. All competitors took part in the new Land Rover Ninety, with support crews using the One Ten.

Borneo presented an extreme jungle challenge beginning at the coastal city of Samarinda in the middle of the rainy season. It was a particularly wet year and the trucks spent so much time underwater that they became known as 'Yellow Submarines'.

Rafting became key to completing the stages. One of the most iconic moments of the event's history came when a heavy-lift helicopter was called in to carry the vehicles to safety when a washed-away road became impassable. The vehicles had to be partly dismantled to be within the helicopter's lift capacity.

It had been an incredibly challenging Camel Trophy which ended in the coastal city of Balikpapan after being re-routed several times. On one day the convoy advanced just 300m after hours and hours of gruelling work.
(Ref: roverparts.com)

abandonment – before transporting it to another mechanic where it was given a new exhaust, timing belt and brakes overhaul, as well as reconditioned fuel pump and injectors from a specialist in Turin. Other minor repairs were carried out to ensure the truck was safe and reliable.

Finally, it was time to address the bodywork. Another good friend who already works on Paolo's other classic vehicles was entrusted with this project because he understands Paolo's attention to detail and very specific requirements.

Following the philosophy of Adam Bennet who restored the 1955 Oxford and 1954 Cambridge Series Ones, he decided to retain as much of the vehicle's patina as possible, preserving the dents, scratches and imperfections which had become an

> 'One of the most iconic moments of the event's history came when a heavy-lift helicopter was called in to carry the vehicles to safety'

important part of its special story.

The body was lightly polished leaving most of the dents in place, only straightening part of the wings to allow re-installation of the wheel arches. Interior trims were removed, cleaned and refitted and the rear sliding windows were replaced. ➲

After the Borneo event, the Ninety was used in Italy for future Camel Trophy team selections

Reconditioned fuel pump and injectors helped the 12J engine to run smoothly again

The bodywork was lightly polished to retain the character of the historic patina

'The body was lightly polished leaving most of the dents in place'

Paolo sourced new old stock XCL Michelin tyres thanks to another good friend and fellow collector Sebastien Conte from France.

Replacement cloth seats were impossible to find so the originals were dismantled, cleaned and repaired by a seamstress from Paolo's village who did a fantastic job.

The finishing touches were the bull bar, winch cradle, roll cage and roof rack which were sandblasted, powder-coated and refitted, drawing to a close a busy five months during which the dignity and grandeur of this 37-year-old Ninety had been reinstated.

After the Borneo event in 1985, the Ninety returned to the UK and was bought by an Italian company that managed Italian ex-Camel Trophy cars and was subsequently used as training for the next event. Later, in 1996 the Ninety was sold, privately, to the same owner who kept it until it passed to Paolo 25 years later. Last July, Paolo managed to reunite the vehicle with one of its event drivers, Beppe Gualini.

The meeting was very emotional for Beppe who hadn't seen the Ninety for almost 30 years. He expressed to Paolo his relief on seeing the quality and sensitivity of the restoration that Paolo had undertaken, appreciating the non-invasive methods used and the careful selection and restoration of original parts. Needless to say Paolo is extremely proud of this very special truck. **CLR**

ABOVE: An emotional reunion with Beppe Gualini, one of the original Italian team members; BELOW: Post-restoration, driving local lanes in northern Italy

ACKNOWLEDGEMENTS

Paolo wishes to thank all those who helped with sourcing parts for this restoration, especially Sebastien Conte (France), Hugh Connolly (Ireland), Darren Brocklehurst (England), Peter Thiebaut (Belgium), Laurens de Smet (Holland), Ezechiel Busuttil (Malta) who supplied big side mirror brackets after a three-weeks search through Maltese scrapyards, and finally Daniel Prasetyo (Indonesia) who recreated the original plate installed for the Borneo competition.

Old Number

After a brief appearance at a Land Rover Series One Club event in 1998, many thought that the first production Land Rover would never see the road again, but fortunately, they were wrong

ONE

The new 4x4 Land Rover was revealed in 1948 and in those 'export or die' days would revive the Rover Company's fortunes in the immediate post-war period when rationing and austerity were constant reminders of the recent conflict.

The Land Rover was one of numerous post-war marvels that paved the way to a more prosperous future thanks to the vehicle's almost immediate success. The first production Land Rover was the first in a range of 'go anywhere' vehicles that, in one form or another, is still being manufactured more than 75 years later. The story started with the 48 pre-production 'pre-pro' prototypes made by Rover, of which the most famous is HUE 166, the first pre-pro.

Once the specification for the new machine was finalised, mass production could start at number one, with the vehicle given the chassis number R860001.

This 80in, the first production Land Rover lay abandoned on a County Durham farm for decades

The aim was to conserve as much of the original vehicle as possible

A painstaking replica of the original hand-punched grille badge

The restored 80in won its class at the Hampton Court concours d'elegance

Dispatched on July 19, 1948, as the factory's records prove, the first production Land Rover was intended for presentation to King George VI but ended up working on farms and mining sites in north-east England.

A decision was made to postpone the presentation and instead, 'number one' was retained by the factory for another 18 months until 1950 when it was registered JUE 477 before leaving the Rover Company's ownership.

Its first custodian was Scot Ewen McEwen (1916-1973), a friend of the Wilks brothers, Maurice and Spencer, who had designed and engineered the Land Rover. This explains why the Land Rover went to the northeast as, at the time, McEwen was professor of agricultural engineering at the University of Durham from 1947 to 1954. The fact that he chose a Land Rover speaks volumes. McEwen was educated in Edinburgh at Merchiston and University College London.

He served his graduate apprenticeship with David Brown and Sons of Huddersfield and rose there to be assistant works manager. His war service as lieutenant colonel and subsequently as assistant director of the Department of Tank Design and assistant chief engineer of the Fighting Vehicles Design Department set the pattern for much of his later career.

After his spell at the University of Durham, successive appointments included director of the armament research and development establishment at Fort Halstead (1955-58), director of engineering with Massey Ferguson Ltd (1958-1963),

JUE 477 as recovered from
Northumberland in 2017

managing director of the Hobourn Group (1965- 67) and finally as vice-chairman (engineering) of Joseph Lucas Ltd from 1967 until his retirement in 1980.

After 20 years of hard use including a spell being used for agricultural training purposes, in December 1970, the ageing workhorse was sold to a Northumberland farmer called David Fairless.

He paid just £15, a sum the farmer remembered as, "the proper price to pay for an old derelict Land-Rover at the time." Fairless wasn't sure whether to continue using the vehicle on his farm in Stanhope, County Durham or to break it up for spares.

Before long, 860001 lay forgotten and exposed to the elements on the farm. Despite this, in 1998, Fairless trailered it 190 miles to Shugborough Hall, in Staffordshire, to attend the Land Rover Series One Club's rally marking the 50th anniversary of the marque.

Despite the Land Rover's ruinous state, 860001 attracted such attention that when

'In 1998, Fairless trailered it 190 miles to Shugborough Hall to attend the Land Rover Series One Club's rally'

Although a 1948 build, the 80in left the factory in 1950 as an updated car in Deep Bronze Green with a core plug engine

'It was to be painstakingly restored by a dedicated team of experts led by chief restorer Julian Shoolheifer'

Fairless got it back home to his farm, he hid the vehicle in a barn. He then barricaded it in behind an assortment of hay bales and vehicle parts but sadly, never found the time to restore 860001 so it remained in the stone barn for a further 19 years.

Following the death of David Fairless, the Land Rover was sold to Sir Jim Ratcliffe, founder and chairman of Ineos, in 2017. It had undoubtedly seen better days, but thanks to the determination of Sir Jim the future of JUE 477 would be secured.

It was to be painstakingly restored by a dedicated team of experts led by chief restorer Julian Shoolheifer under the watchful eye of Andrew Nahum, keeper emeritus at the Science Museum.

The emphasis was on retaining its patina and re-using as much of its original material and as many parts as possible, something that unsurprisingly, many said couldn't be done.

Over the next two years, Shoolheifer set about restoring the vehicle while retaining 'as much of its original DNA as was physically, and safely, possible' and crucially, making sure that this remarkable vehicle's history and past life was still worn with pride.

The restoration team had to address the Land Rover's history in the two years between being built and being sold by the factory. Of this, Shoolheifer said: "For the record, 001 left the factory in 1950 as an updated car in Deep Bronze Green with a core plug engine. It also had the early screen updated with trafficator brackets."

Of the completed project Shoolheifer explained, "We returned the restored JUE-y to the Northumberland farm from which we'd rescued it in 2017 and took it across two miles of peat bog tracks taking it home once more. Off-road in really tough conditions it performed superbly.

"We showed it no mercy. It was restored to be used. To be able to drive Land Rover 0001 through wind, rain, sun and snow on those same roads it had travelled nearly 50 years before is one of the greatest experiences of my life."

Others shared Shoolheifer's enthusiasm as, on its first outing, JUE 477 won the 1940s class at the 2020 Concours of Elegance at Hampton Court Palace in London - one of the world's celebrated showpiece events for classic and vintage cars.

It returned to Hampton Court Palace for a fourth consecutive year in 2020, after previous years at Windsor Castle, St James' Palace in London and at the Palace of Holyroodhouse in Edinburgh.

As well as bringing together a selection of 60 of the rarest cars from around the world to compete in the concours, hundreds of other fine motor cars were displayed by car clubs in a bid to win the Club Trophy. JUE 477's presence was supported by several other historic 4x4s, including a fully restored 1980 Toyota FJ40 Land Cruiser, a 1944 Willys Jeep

Original registration is still valid

in US Navy colours and a classic 1988 Mercedes-Benz G-Wagen.

The first Ineos Grenadier prototype was also displayed and while to some, this new 4x4 is controversial, it is down to its founder's enthusiasm that JUE 477 has been returned to roadworthiness. Of that roadworthiness and its future, Shoolheifer said: "It must be remembered it is privately owned. I very much expect it will be used as intended.

"It was driven through central London to Hampton Court to the Concours via the A3 on Thursday and back on Sunday night mixing with city traffic.

"It'll probably get used around the lanes and for beach and pub adventures. It's a cracker on the road, drives very nicely and sings along." **CLR**

Six Ferries TO **Six Nations**

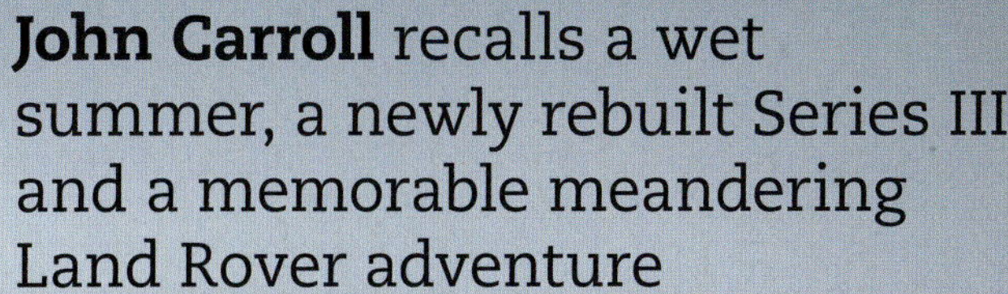

John Carroll recalls a wet summer, a newly rebuilt Series III and a memorable meandering Land Rover adventure

WORDS **JOHN CARROLL** PHOTOS **JOHN AND RO CARROLL**

While many classic Land Rover owners dream of overland trips to exotic places, it's not always possible. Reality gets in the way of daydreams and we often have to do what we can in a fortnight or less.

To complicate things, we also want to use our Land Rovers on holiday rather than leaving them at home. Faced with such a dilemma one year, Ro and I planned a trip that would allow us to remain relatively close to home but go on a fortnight's trip to places we'd not been to before.

To make the trip memorable we decided that we'd visit parts of all the countries and islands that comprise the United Kingdom and the Republic of Ireland, hence the loose description of the adventure as 'six nations' and there would

'I knew that I had to have it and put in a bid big enough to ensure I'd win it'

also be six ferry crossings.

We'd cover much of the distance involved on some of those ferries rather than aboard aeroplanes, which meant we could go in one of my old Land Rovers. The question was which one? In reality, there was just one choice, the Abersoch Express, a Searle Safari that, back then, was just about finished.

How it got that name is worth a few words of explanation. While it was still in the workshop, I was washing my Series One on the drive outside my mum and dad's house on the Wirral. A woman with a posh accent, walking her dog, passing the time of day said: "We had one of those many years ago and used it to tow our boat to Abersoch."

Abersoch, on the Llyn peninsula of North Wales, is about 100 miles by road from the Wirral peninsula and has long been a weekend playground for the well-heeled sailing crowd. It clicked immediately. One reason I'd bought the 1973 Series III camper was that its 1970s style reminded me of memorable childhood camping weekends that always seemed to be sunny. It was still being welded at the time and I promised myself that I'd drive it to Abersoch when it was finished.

Thinking back to the Land Rovers I have owned over the past 30 years or so, it seems that most of them have been bought as almost derelict sheds and turned into functional Land Rovers as magazine project vehicles. The subject of this story is an example of just such a purchase made a decade ago.

After hours in a Croydon office one evening, I was idly browsing Land Rovers on eBay and stumbled on this Limestone-painted, 88in Series III. It didn't sound particularly exciting except for one tiny detail, it was listed as a Searle camper. Searle of Sunbury-on-Thames was the company behind the famous Carawagon conversions. The short-wheelbase Carawagons are even rarer than their long-wheelbase counterparts and there were two kinds, SWB Carawagons and Safari Sleepers.

The latter, as their name suggested, offered sleeping accommodation but weren't as well-appointed as the full Carawagons with their cookers and cupboards. The one I was looking at was a Safari Sleeper that was pretty rough, rusty and missing its bespoke interior. I knew that I had to have it and put in a bid big enough to ensure I'd win it then went to the pub to ponder on what I'd done.

Subsequently, the Safari Sleeper's rebirth from an abandoned rust bucket to a functional camper was comprehensively documented in a magazine's workshop pages. Tony Sinclair at Alldrive repaired the chassis, fitted a 300Tdi, a set of parabolic springs and, for a bit of '70s custom 'vanning' style, a porthole and a set of repainted Weller eight-spoke wheels. Otherwise, it is pretty standard with its original Series III gearbox and differentials.

Back on the Wirral, my dad's careful joinery recreated the missing seats/beds, I got them upholstered and it was suddenly time to take it to the popular coastal seaside resort that had given it its nickname pretty much by accident during this

process. Abersoch, our final destination, might be on North Wales' Llyn peninsula but we'd head there via a peculiar route.

It started raining as we rattled up the Wirral on the M53 towards the ferry terminal in Birkenhead's docks. As the shakedown run for an untested truck, rebuilt from a very dilapidated Series III with mostly used and recycled stuff, it was going to be rather demanding.

Onboard the overnight ferry to Belfast, the MV Stena Mersey, that would carry us westwards to Northern Ireland, we sank a Guinness or two before crawling into our bunks. The schedule meant that time in Northern Ireland was limited and it was still raining as we disembarked and headed to a dockside café for an Ulster fry.

We met up with James Wylie, also a Series III owner to compare our rebuilt 88in Land Rovers by the new Titanic Belfast building, a stone's throw from the yard where the RMS Titanic was built a century earlier. With the rain lashing down, we beat a hasty retreat into the centre of Belfast and had a stroll around City Hall.

It's a quick turnaround, so before long we

Split oil pipe, Kirkcudbright, Scotland

Douglas, IOM

Shannon Ferry, ROI

Belfast, NI

were queueing to board the Stena Line ferry back across the Irish Sea to Scotland, nation number two, and wondering why so much water was getting inside the Land Rover.

I'd sealed the panes of the screen before we left, but we had leaks of Titanic proportions somewhere and our feet were soaked. A couple of hours later we disembarked at Cairnryan. It was still pouring down and a tiring run to Dumfries,

Isle of Man green lane

Peel Castle, IOM

'The Safari Sleeper's rebirth from abandoned rust bucket to the functional camper was comprehensively documented in a magazine's workshop pages'

75 miles down the A75, followed. The coastal scenery was completely masked by the weather and the front nearside sidelight and indicator failed, so the warmth of the hotel was welcome.

The next morning, I asked the RAC man to look at the electrics and we got the failed lights working before heading to the coast at Kirkcudbright. Suddenly, my feet were wet again but this time the liquid was hot and black. It was engine oil. Investigation showed that the rubber pipe from the oil cooler to the engine had split. I wiped it with kitchen roll and bodged it with duct tape and cable ties and, although it proved oil-tight, back at the motel, I reflected that I had had much better starts to a trip.

Sunday was nation number three, the Isle of Man, so we headed back into England and ran south in the sunshine to Heysham and the Isle of Man Steam Packet Co ferry terminal. Except for a couple of checks

Tully, Co Kildare, ROI

Barry's Tea? Must be Ireland

of the bodged pipe and the oil level, the Carawagon ate up the miles south without drama. It didn't sound stressed at all and kept up a steady 55-60mph pace.

I was beginning to see the value of the Tdi engine conversion for use in Series Land Rovers. Even so, I was relieved that the 88in hadn't let us down again because missing the ferry would have

seriously interfered with onward travel. It was an afternoon crossing aboard the Ben-my-Chree, that landed us at our fourth destination, at one end of the prom in Douglas. The prom is a couple of miles long, lined with hotels – including ours – and, during the summer, filled with horse-drawn trams.

It's been a stressful start to the trip, so

FERRIES

Birkenhead to Belfast
www.stenaline.co.uk

Belfast to Cairnryan
www.stenaline.co.uk

Heysham to Douglas
www.steam-packet.com

Douglas to Dublin
www.steam-packet.com

Shannon Ferry
www.shannonferries.com

Rosslare to Fishguard
www.stenaline.co.uk

Kinsale, Co Cork, ROI

Camping in Killarney, ROI

Sneem, ROI

Inch Beach, Co Cork, ROI

having Monday for sightseeing on the Isle of Man was a real treat. I checked the oil, went to a motor factors for some rubber oil pipe for fitting later and then we behaved like the holidaymakers we were for the rest of the day. We drove down to Calf Sound at the south of the island to watch seals through the binoculars, meandered along a green lane for a picnic, walked along a coastal footpath, had ice cream by Peel Castle and finally had a pint in The Crosby on the TT motorcycle racing circuit on the way back to Douglas.

We were due to leave this relaxed island early the next morning, and the ferry Manannan was about to start boarding when we arrived.

It sailed on time and was our fourth ferry crossing of the trip. We were bound for Dublin, the 'old country', and the fifth 'nation', the Republic of Ireland. The ferry terminal isn't far from the mouth of the River Liffey and Dublin's city centre. We plunged into the city's traffic and, not for the first time, the enhanced visibility afforded by the porthole window in the

'A 300Tdi engine and parabolic springs turn a Series III into a 'leaf-sprung Defender'

blind hard-top made it easier to cope with the city's frenetic traffic.

I'd been to Dublin plenty of times and with a surname like Carroll, it's hard not to feel at home there. I showed Ro as many of the city's sights as we could squeeze in including the statues of Molly Malone and Phil Lynott, the General Post Office where the Easter Rising started in 1916, Trinity College and more. We viewed historic buildings from an open-top bus and ended up in the tourist pubs of Temple Bar drinking Guinness and listening to the fiddle tunes.

There are new motorways across Ireland now and, eager to get to the west coast, we took the M7 to Limerick, from where we were planning to slow things down by spending a whole week between there and Rosslare.

From Limerick, we headed on to Killimer and the Shannon Car Ferry that took us to the south bank of the mighty river on which transatlantic flying boats landed in the 1940s. From there, we headed south through Listowel and Tralee to Killarney in time to pitch the tent before it rained again.

I had fixed an awning strip to the rear of the Land Rover so we could connect a Movelite camper van awning. As we'd be there for three nights, we opted to pitch the awning for sitting and cooking in and a smaller dome tent for sleeping.

With the weather alternating between rain and sunshine throughout the week, we made the best of it and on successive days drove out to see the area. We headed to Dingle and along the beach at Inch and on another day, we drove through Molls Gap and around much of the Ring of Kerry, the scenic route around the Iveragh peninsula in Co Kerry.

This circular route takes in rugged and verdant coastal landscapes and rural seaside villages and is roughly 100 miles around. We stopped in Sneem

Peel Castle
Isle of Man
Glasgow
Edinburgh
Cairnryan
Kirkcudbright
Dumfries
Carlisle
SCOTLAND
NORTHERN
IRELAND
LOUGH NEAGH
Belfast
Lough Erne
REPUBLIC
OF
IRELAND
R. SHANNON
Peel
Castle
Douglas
ISLE
OF
MAN
Heysham
IRISH SEA
DUBLIN
M7
Birkenhead
Ennis
Lough Derg
Lough Ree
Pwllheli
PORTHMADOG
Birmingham
Killimer
Limerick
Wexford
Abersoch
Aberystwyth
R. SHANNON FERRY
Tarbert
Listowel
Waterford
Aberaeron
Devils
Bridge
Vale of
Rheidol
Railway
Tregaron
Inch
Beach
Tralee
Killarney
Cork
Rosslare
Llanerchaeron
Dingle
Macroom
Dungarvan
FISHGUARD
London
Iveragh
Peninsula
Moll's Gap
Killarney
Kenmare
KIRKCUDBRIGHT
SCOTLAND
Sneem
Kinsale
Ring of
Kerry
WALES
ENGLAND
Wales
Co. Kerry, Ireland

Dungarvan, ROI

the brand-new clutch slave cylinder failed so I had to call the RAC for the second time on this trip. Luckily and possibly because we were in an area where Land Rovers are part of the scenery, the RAC man arrived with a new slave cylinder. He fitted it in double-quick time and we were back on the road to the campsite.

By the next morning, the torrential rain that had dogged much of the trip returned and, with a Land Rover already loaded with wet gear, there was little enthusiasm for another night under canvas. The Travelodge in Porthmadog had plenty of cheap rooms available so we took advantage of the big beds and warm showers.

The next morning's TV news included flood warnings for the area. We headed up through Pwllheli to Abersoch which wasn't much fun in the rain knowing that the long haul back to Yorkshire awaited us so set off home earlier than we probably would have done. Peering through the flat screen at the rain-soaked tarmac of the A499 and the A55, it was evident that the Abersoch Express was, despite the teething troubles and clutch slave cylinder failure, a great success.

It was just as evident that, despite what

and Kenmare. In the latter, we had a pint in the Tom Crean pub which is named after an unsung hero of three major British expeditions to the Antarctic at the beginning of the 20th century. It is reported that Crean spent more time in the ice and snow than the more celebrated figures of Sir Ernest Shackleton and Capt Robert Scott. For these exploits, he was awarded the Polar Medal and for his actions on one, he was also awarded the Albert Medal for Lifesaving, a British medal which has since been replaced by the George Cross.

On our third day, we headed over to Kinsale and on these journeys on twisting country roads, I became convinced that a 300Tdi engine and parabolic springs turn a Series III into a 'leaf-sprung Defender'. The next morning, in line with our schedule, we packed up and headed eastwards through Macroom and Cork to Dungarvan, still dodging the rain and meandering around places of interest. A B&B in the harbour town of Dungarvan was warm and dry and the Guinness in one of the town's bars was cold and wet.

The Irish leg of the trip was drawing to a close ahead of the sixth and final ferry crossing and the sixth nation, Wales. En route to Rosslare, there was time to visit Waterford where reflecting different interests, we went shopping in places as diverse as Waterford Harley-Davidson and

Series IIIs near Kenmare, ROI

the Waterford Crystal shop. That afternoon, we mooched around Wexford which is just half an hour's drive from the ferry terminal in Rosslare from where we'd make the crossing with Stena Line to Fishguard.

Dublin to Holyhead might be the obvious choice to get to Abersoch but we opted to drive up the coastal route along Cardigan Bay and camped for a couple of nights near Aberaeron.

We had a run out from the campsite and went to the National Trust property Llanerchaeron which is described as 'an elegant Georgian villa, set in the wooded Aeron valley. Remarkably unaltered for over 200 years, this self-sufficient estate includes a farm, walled gardens and lake.'

We dodged the showers with cake and coffee in the cafe before heading up to Tregaron and Devil's Bridge. At the latter, we watched the Vale of Rheidol steam train arrive at the station after the long pull up the incline from Aberystwyth. That afternoon en route back to the campsite

Morfa Bychan, Wales

turned out to be one of the wettest summers on record, the six-nation tour, with its theme of islands, peninsulas and ferries, was also a great success. It proved that there is plenty of scope for fortnight-long Land Rover adventures in Britain and Ireland.

It's a theme that offers numerous possibilities around the Celtic islands, especially in Scotland – there are plenty more ferry crossings – and before we got anywhere near the Pennine hills and home, we were already thinking about another trip.

'This circular route takes in rugged and verdant coastal landscapes and rural seaside villages'

While this Land Rover is ideal for such trips, the next time we went to Ireland in a Land Rover it was to be in a Series One to attend the Land Rover Series One Club's annual rally.

The Abersoch Express subsequently proved its worth on two-week trips to Holland, Spain and Portugal as well as numerous weekend ones in the UK. I find that it's easy to use with the dome tent-like Movelite awning when camping with two people.

It can be cosy to sleep in when I am using it by myself because, although it will accommodate two people, there isn't much room for their gear. In conjunction with a Trangia stove, it excels as, what the Americans would term a 'day van', for greenlaning, canoeing and just meandering around the countryside. Among my various Land Rover projects, it's been a great success and although, after 13 years it is ready for a gentle bit of cosmetic refurbishment, it's a keeper. **CLR**

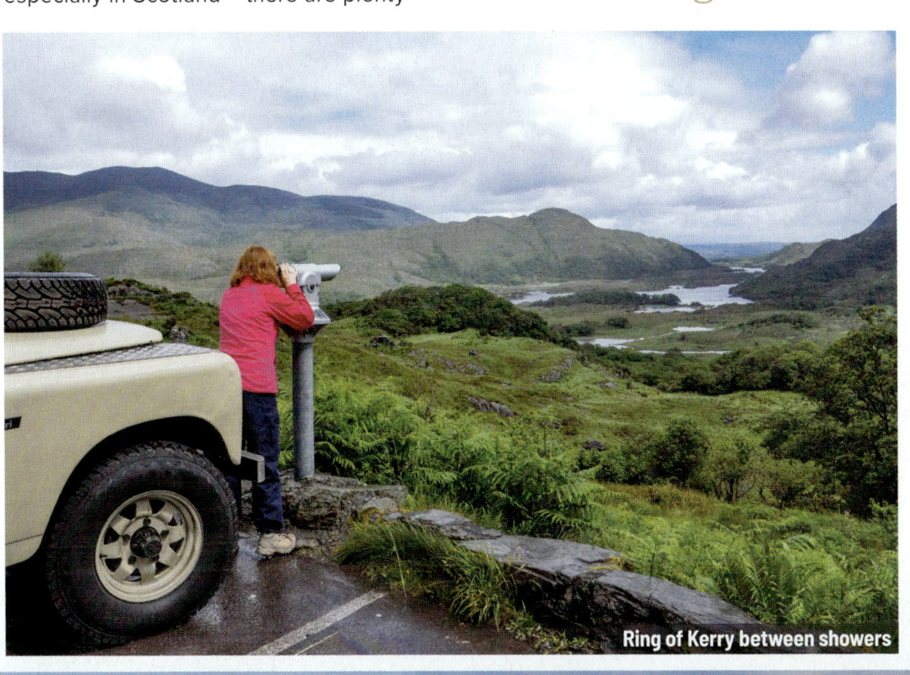

Ring of Kerry between showers

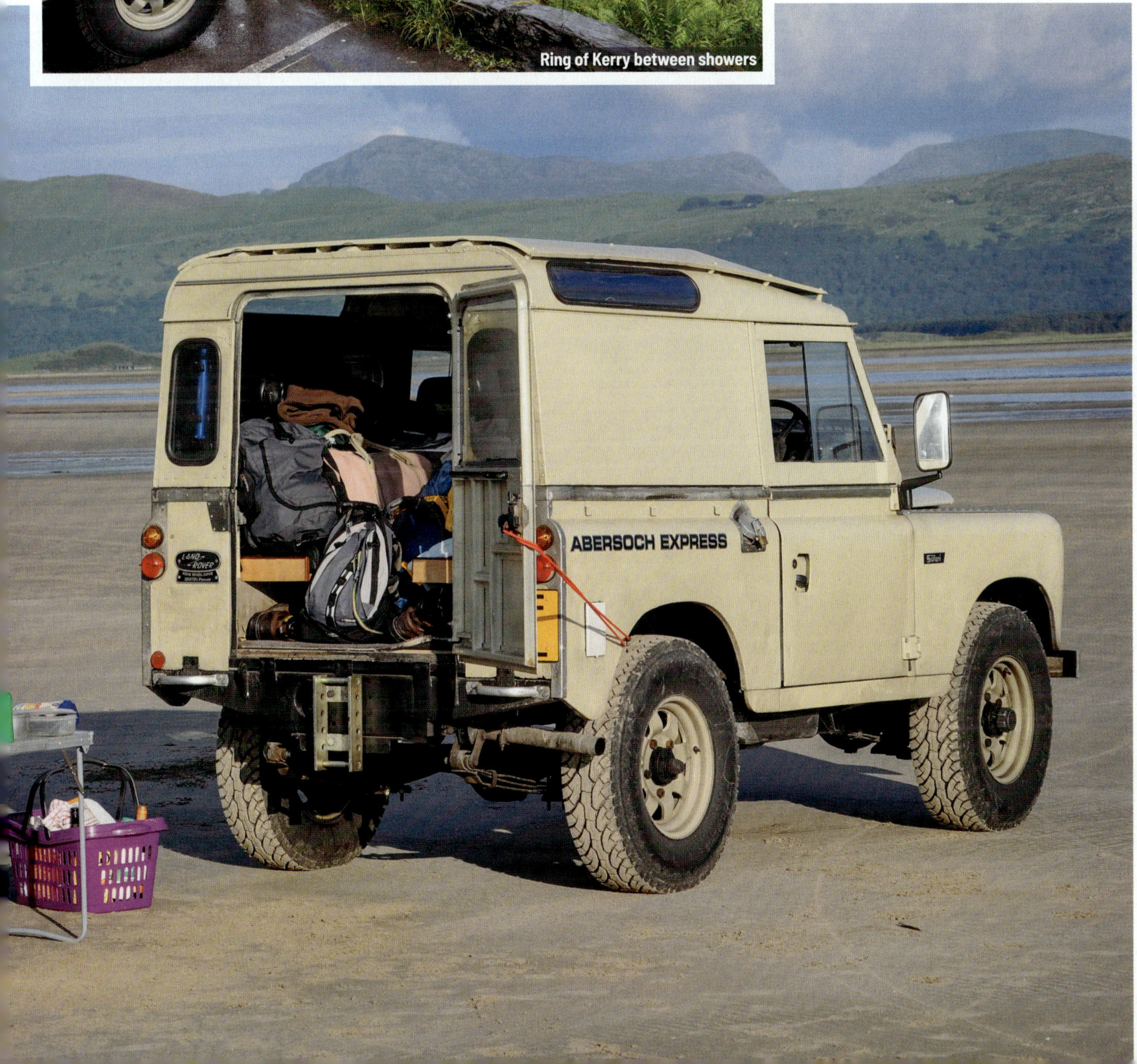

Millennium *Falcon*

Cevat Vardarli asks Orkan Sahin of Falcon
Design Germany about his company's
phenomenal restoration of an 88in Series III

WORDS **CEVAT VARDARLI**
PHOTOS **FALCON DESIGN GERMANY**

Where does your interest in Land Rovers come from?

I like SUVs. As a daily driver I have a Range Rover Vogue, but you specifically ask why I like Land Rovers so much. I like the community of really cool people who also like to drive their cars. I don't like people who buy cars and make them into 'parking lot queens'. A car is there to drive!

When did you start your business with cars? Can you describe your career until now?

It was 2003 when I started to build up my own business. First I opened a car dealership in Köln, where I bought cheap and broken cars to repair and sell them again for a low price. I am a car mechanic so I had no problems doing that. This is also where my passion for the used car trade started. In the following years, I increased my budget more and moved towards luxury cars. Gradually, I also got many famous customers all around the world who wanted a car from me. In 2017 I started a collaboration with 'Automobile - The Car Magazine' on German VOX TV where I show the viewers how I buy special cars from around the world and how to ship them back to Germany.

The galvanised chassis before the vehicle's build

A brand-new bulkhead was fabricated

When did you create Falcon Design Germany?

I started Falcon Design Germany in 2017, not very long after Land Rover had announced that it would stop producing the classic Defender.

This meant it was the perfect moment to start the new brand Falcon Design Germany with a passion for restored Land Rovers. We also have other classic cars but our main business is Land Rovers. The company is based in Cologne, Germany, and the factory where we build our cars is in Izmir, Turkey.

On the subject of classic Land Rovers, can you tell us what led to the restoration of this blue 88in Series III?

Sure, we build our cars to order and this Series III was built for a doctor here in Germany. First, we bought a vehicle that

Many new panels were made from scratch

Modern components used in wiring

Fully reconditioned
2,286cc petrol engine

Marine Blue goes on in
Falcon's paintshop

Painted tub and new
floor supports

Freshly painted rear tub

would be a good basis for the project. We need to get a chassis without too much rust or any damaged parts. The body is not so important to us because we will make it all new from scratch. The bodywork is handmade in our factory. After sandblasting the chassis we repair the rusty parts and hot-dip galvanise the chassis to protect it from rust for future years. Once we have this base to build on we can start properly. We overhaul the front and rear axles, differentials, and brake components and put new brake pipes and hoses on it. We also overhaul the complete engine and, in this Land Rover, you'll find the original 2,286cc engine. At the same time, others in our team produce the body parts for the restoration. We make 80% of the parts from aluminium just like the original parts and only the bulkhead, radiator panel and rear tailgate are not made from aluminium. We also change the wiring harness and fuse box to incorporate more modern components. In the end, the complete process usually takes us around three months.

Where did this Land Rover come from? What is its year of production and was it your car or a customer's?

This is a 1974 Series III. We build our cars to order, that's why it's our car when the project starts and the customer gets it after the restoration is finished. We buy our cars from Italy, Greece and Turkey. We restore and rebuild Series III Long and Short models as well as the Land Rover 90 and 110 models.

What condition was it before the restoration?

There was no serious damage to the car, the chassis was in good shape but the body parts were corroded and in some parts such as the bulkhead, we had holes to deal with. The engine was running well but the exhaust was rusty and holed so it didn't sound good.

The work on this restoration makes the vehicle look like new. Was it a request from a customer or work you felt necessary on a vehicle to be sold?

We do only full restorations and we do our best to make the Series III better than the factory's finish.

Where did you start?

We have a 12-person team at Falcon Design, and everyone specialises in one craft, so we start everything at the same time and work progresses in parallel.

How did you recreate the body panels?

This took us a long time to research. We had to find parts in good shape to take measurements from but now it's no longer difficult to produce parts made to the original measurements because we clone them 1:1.

This Series III was built for a German doctor

The rebuilt rear axle in situ

What were the most difficult tasks during the process?

When we started in 2017, our biggest problem was finding body parts for the Series III, so we started to make our own. We also sell parts for clients who need them for our restoration projects.

How long did it take?

To finish a Series III after a client makes an order takes us three months.

About the overhauling of the engine, could you give me a list of the new parts fitted?

Every engine goes through an overhauling process in our factory. First, we open the engine up to see its condition. The basic process is that we change the bearings, pistons and rings, carburettor and fuel system, cooling system including radiator and the hoses, new filters, fuel pipes and fuel tank. Before we put all the parts together we repaint the engine in our shade of blue we also coat the engine manifold with special heat-resistant paint.

Displayed at Retro Classic in Stuttgart, Germany

Seat colour was chosen by customer

Natural wood decking

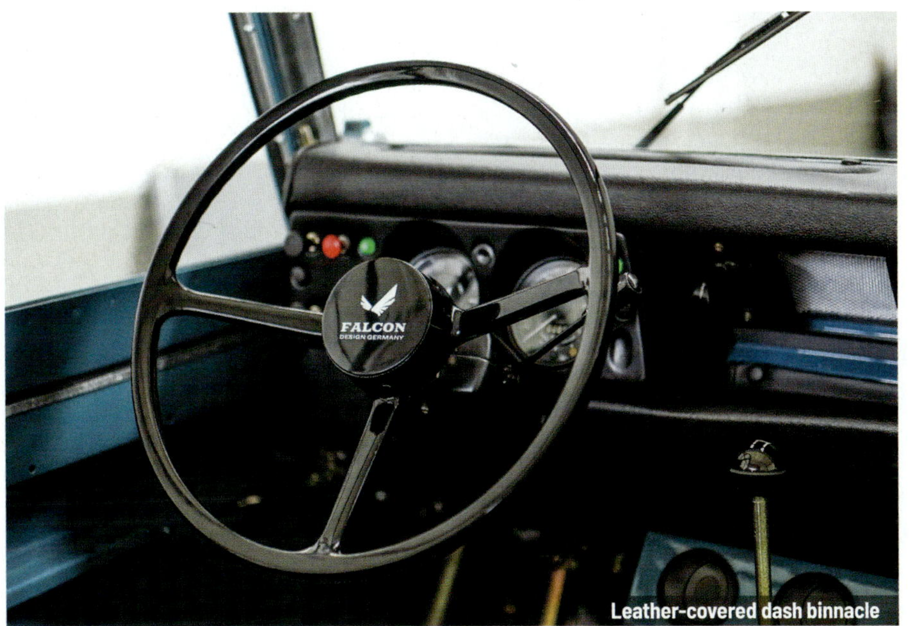

Leather-covered dash binnacle

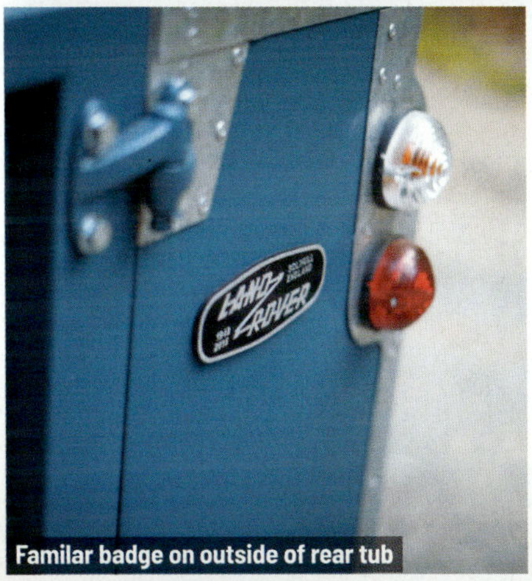

Familar badge on outside of rear tub

'This is a 1974 Series III. We build our cars to order, that's why it's our car when the project starts'

What work did you do to the suspension?
We use the original leaf springs; first, we disassemble all parts for sandblasting so we clean all the rust from the surfaces. After this, we paint or powder coat parts as necessary. Before we reassemble it all, we ask our clients, what level of comfort they want in the suspension, a hard or a softer, more comfortable ride? Because not all of our customers will want to use their vehicles on the land or in natural environments we can change the leaf springs set up to make it comfortable for street and daily use.

Do you do the leather upholstery yourself? Was it the customer who chose this caramel leather in this Land Rover?
Yes, in our factory we also have a car upholstery division. We do all restorations to order so every client can make their own Series III individual. It was the client's request for caramel leather for the front and back seats. The dashboard is also finished with caramel leather but we have also supplied black upholstery.

Tell me about the wooden floor in the back.
The wood floor in the back of this Series III was the one thing not made in our factory. We asked a factory that specialises in wooden decking for boats and yachts to make that for us. **CLR**

MORE INFORMATION
www.falcondesigngermany.com

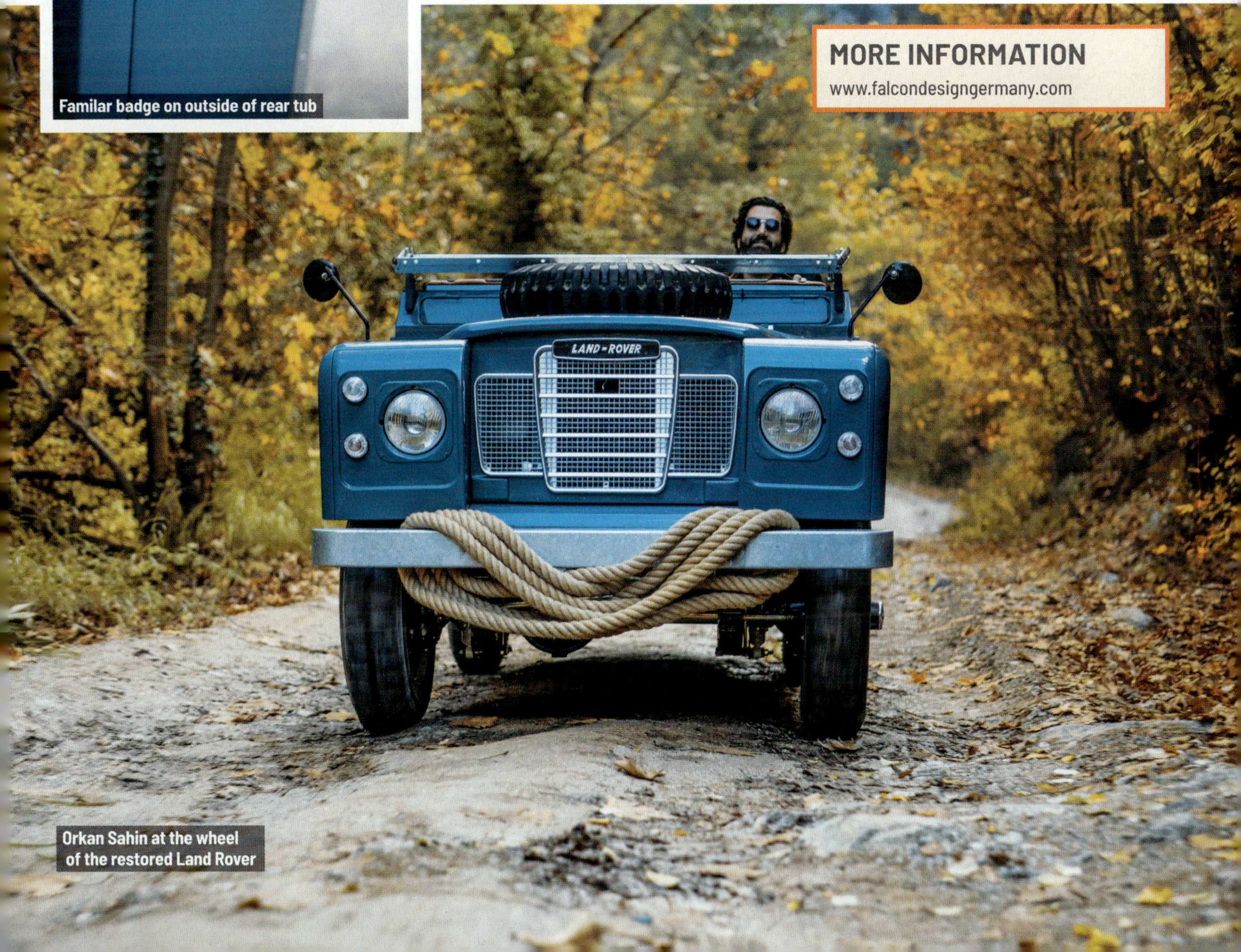

Orkan Sahin at the wheel of the restored Land Rover

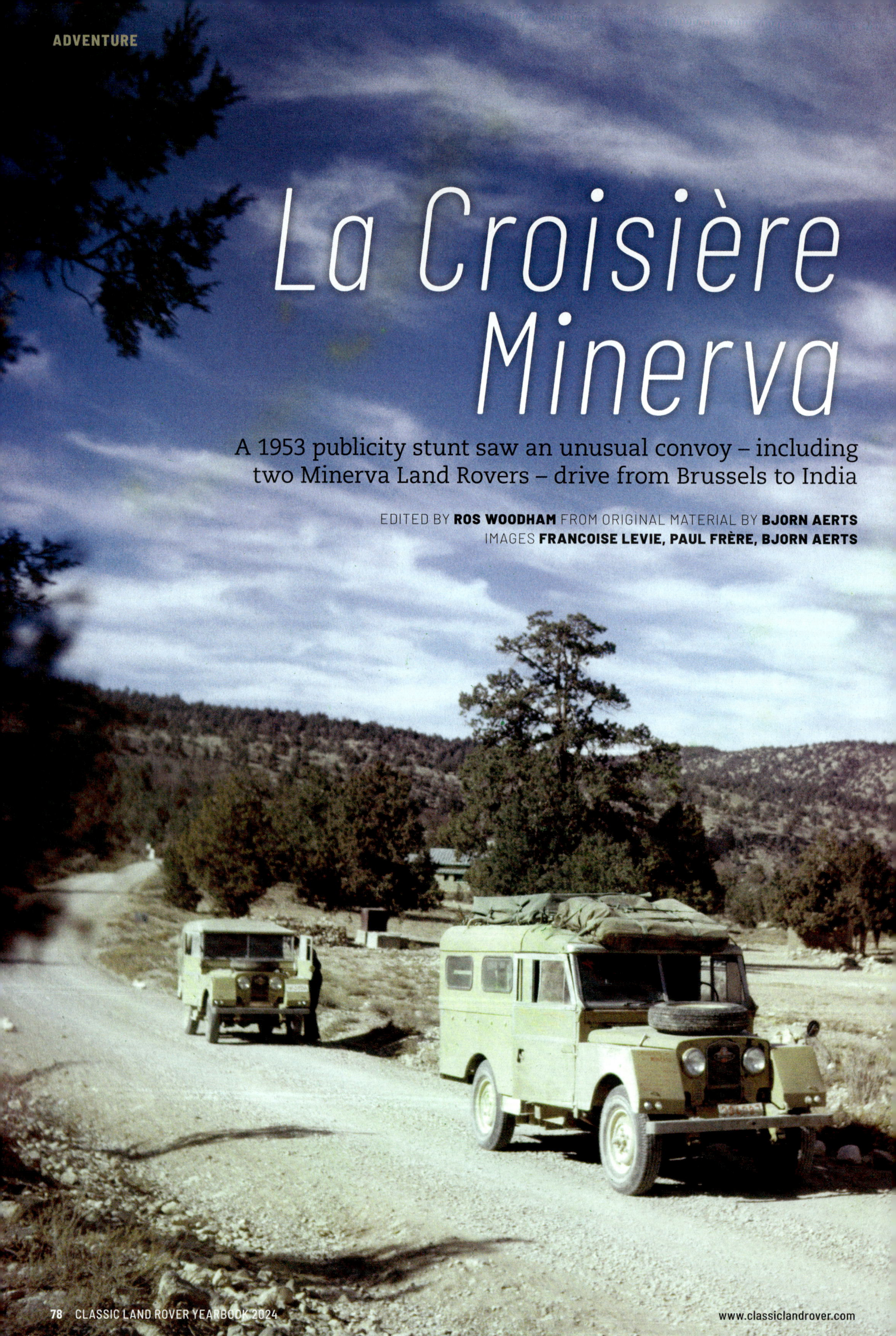

La Croisière Minerva

A 1953 publicity stunt saw an unusual convoy – including two Minerva Land Rovers – drive from Brussels to India

EDITED BY **ROS WOODHAM** FROM ORIGINAL MATERIAL BY **BJORN AERTS**
IMAGES **FRANCOISE LEVIE, PAUL FRÈRE, BJORN AERTS**

After World War Two, Société Nouvelle Minerva, founded in 1935 by automobile entrepreneur Mathieu Van Roggen, faced challenges in restarting motor vehicle assembly in its bombed-out Mortsel factory near Antwerp, Belgium. In 1951, the Belgian defence forces sought lightweight 4x4s, and Van Roggen secured a contract for 2,500 Land Rovers, out-pitching Willys. Belgium supplied steel and parts, aiding production, and by 1953, the assembly plant was producing 25 vehicles per day, completing an order of around 9,000 4x4s.

As the defence contract concluded, Van Roggen shifted focus to civil and export markets, assembling a local version of

Ready for departure from Brussels

the 86in Land Rover under license. To revive Belgian automobile manufacturing, he planned a luxury touring car and opted for local assembly of the Armstrong Siddeley Sapphire 346 saloon car, powered by a 3.4L six-cylinder engine, rivalling the Jaguar MK IV.

Facing funding challenges, Van Roggen approached Raymond Boschmans, vice-president of the Royal Automobile Club of Belgium, known for overland adventures. Boschmans, with diplomatic connections,

organised a 15,000km trip to India. Journalist and avid racing driver Paul Frère drove one Armstrong, writing articles and a book, while Boschmans and his wife travelled in the other. Cinematographer Pierre Levie with his wife Suzette and their son Jean-Pierre, led a film crew for a documentary series on cultural heritage.

Van Roggen supplied Land Rovers for the trip, modifying a 107in pick-up for the film crew. The first 107in, chassis 47230014, arrived in Mortsel on September 4, 1953. Modifications included adding a fuel tank, an electrical generator between the front seats for filming lights and a fabricated hardtop. The second 80in Minerva, possibly a police vehicle, carried film equipment and luggage.

Both Armstrong Siddeley Sapphires had standard specs, one with a roof rack. Philips car radios provided entertainment on the road. Diplomatic passports facilitated border crossings through Yugoslavia, Turkey, Syria, Iraq, Iran, Pakistan, and India.

On October 2, 1953, the vehicles gathered in Brussels, departing to the Dutch border. Overloaded, the Land Rovers handled poorly, prompting a stop in Ulm for rear leaf spring reinforcement.

The journey continued to Salzburg to join the Armstrongs and then eastward to Belgrade, where a reception awaited from the Belgian ambassador. Progressing east, worsening weather and plummeting temperatures challenged the Land Rovers on smaller, deteriorating roads. Floods made some routes impassable, redirecting them from the planned Studenica Monastery stay in Serbia to Skopje, 210km away.

In Mitrovica, the crew found a decent restaurant for the night, indulging in a traditional Yugoslavian breakfast before rejoining the team in Skopje. Dusty gravel tracks led to the Greek border, where

'An unexpected large bump launched the Sapphire into the air'

The 80in and 107in Minerva Land Rovers carried the film crew and their equipment

The expedition members (photo taken in Baghdad)

'The final leg of the journey to New Delhi unfolded without major issues'

conditions were initially favourable. However, torrential rain in Greece made night driving hazardous. Exhausted, they reached Thessaloniki after a week of driving. Having covered 2,960km, they were now beginning to experience more oriental influence in the cuisine and culture.

Director Pierre Levie planned to film Byzantine churches around Thessaloniki for two days, exploring those under restoration since the 1917 fire. Boschmans continued toward Alexandropoulos, but relentless rains forced him to send his Armstrong Siddeley by train to Turkey. Frère and the crew decided to test the route, with Land Rovers leading.

Under persistent rain and winds, they journeyed to the Turkish border, encountering flooded fields, and struggling to keep the Armstrong's spark plugs dry. After a recce, they faced blocked bridges and submerged roads, returning to Alexandropoulos for the night. The following morning they attempted to cross the railway bridge in Souphli, aided by wooden boards.

With the Boschmans' Armstrong finally unloaded from the delayed train they continued through swollen rivers and treacherous roads. Progress slowed to just 90km in six hours. Approaching the Greek border post, muddy roads in no man's land sent the 80in sliding into a ditch. With the combined force of both Land Rovers and a rope, they managed to free the 80in and continue to the Turkish border post.

Covering 280km in darkness, they reached Istanbul for a week of rest and Oriental culture. The luggage rack in the back of the 80in Land Rover had collapsed but otherwise, the vehicles had fared well through the challenging roads of Yugoslavia and Greece. Two days were dedicated to vehicle maintenance, preparing for the next leg of their adventurous journey.

Paul Frère vividly captured the contrasts of Istanbul, where the intersection of east and west, old and new, creates a captivating tapestry. The city's dichotomy includes hardworking beggars alongside opulent Ottoman palaces. After exploring Istanbul, the group divided into two: filmmaker Paul Levie and his crew ventured into Anatolia's countryside and Roman ruins in Land

The full convoy assembled outside a German hotel

The floods washed away the main river crossing in a Turkish valley

Reinforcing rear leaf springs at a garage in Germany

Jean-Pierre Levie talks to locals in Yugoslavia

Levie writes "Croisière Minerva" on the 107in

Rovers, while Frère, the Boschmans and others drove the Armstrong Siddeleys to Ankara for visas and permits.

Levie's team, having visited the Green and Blue Mosque in Bursa, travelled 450km to Izmir. There, the crew split up, with Levie in the 80in heading to Denizli, while Suzette and cinematographer Gérard Perrin filmed the temple of Darius in the 107in. Disaster struck as they sought the perfect filming spot; the 107in overturned after a sharp bend. Suzette, Perrin, and their guide faced injuries, but with local help, they got the Land Rover back on its wheels and towed to Ephesus.

Unable to reach the crew that night, Suzette finally contacted Pierre in the morning. He joined them in Izmir, and after three days of repairs, the Land Rover was ready. Starting at 4am, they aimed to catch up with the expedition. Levie's filming schedule had suffered delays. To complicate matters, en route to Kutaya, they experienced a flat tyre, a failing clutch, and noisy rear wheel bearings. Another garage pit stop and a semi-fitting wheel bearing later, they were ready to resume.

Meanwhile, the rest of the crew explored the Turkish interior, navigating the challenging terrain of the Cappadocian Mountains. Frère marvelled at villages that likely had never seen a motor vehicle, especially a limousine like the Sapphire. They documented Ürgüp and the ancient Hittite site of Göreme, carved into soft rocks since 1200BC.

Jean-Pierre Levie takes a break on the 107in

Meeting the King of Jordan

Sidon Sea Castle, Saida, Lebanon

Desert repairs on a Minerva axle

Levie informed the crew that the 80in would join them in Aleppo to assist in filming. The crew continued on excellent roads through the mountains toward the Syrian border. The adventure pressed on, presenting challenges and unexpected delays, but the allure of exploration and cultural discovery remained undiminished.

Syria marked a stark contrast from Turkey, unfolding with wide, empty landscapes where farmers in traditional Arab attire toiled the fertile, dark red soil with donkeys. Villages comprised whitewashed clay houses and domed-roof grain stores. Driving towards Aleppo under the setting sun's deep orange glow, the crew silently relished the enchantment of their overland adventure.

In Aleppo, they navigated the ancient souks and labyrinthine streets filled with shops and ateliers. A small reception at the Belgian Consul's residence in a 400-year-old palace, amid the souks, included the Boschmans and the Naman family, Syria's Ford agent and importer. The vehicles were given names – Frère's Armstrong became Ali-baba, and Mrs Naman painted the Sapphire's Arabic name on the bonnet. The 107in, later named Ferblantine, joined them after overcoming ignition issues.

After a gruelling 750km, Pierre and Suzette arrived late that night in Adana only to find the 80in stranded there with ignition problems. After a roadside fix, they drove carefully through winding mountain passes, reaching Aleppo exhausted. Frère and the cinematographers headed to Lebanon, stopping at the Crac des

Aleppo street scene, Syria

'Levie and the remaining crew followed the same road the next day'

Pierre Levie and his son Jean-Pierre in front of the ruins of the ancient city of Sardis, Turkey

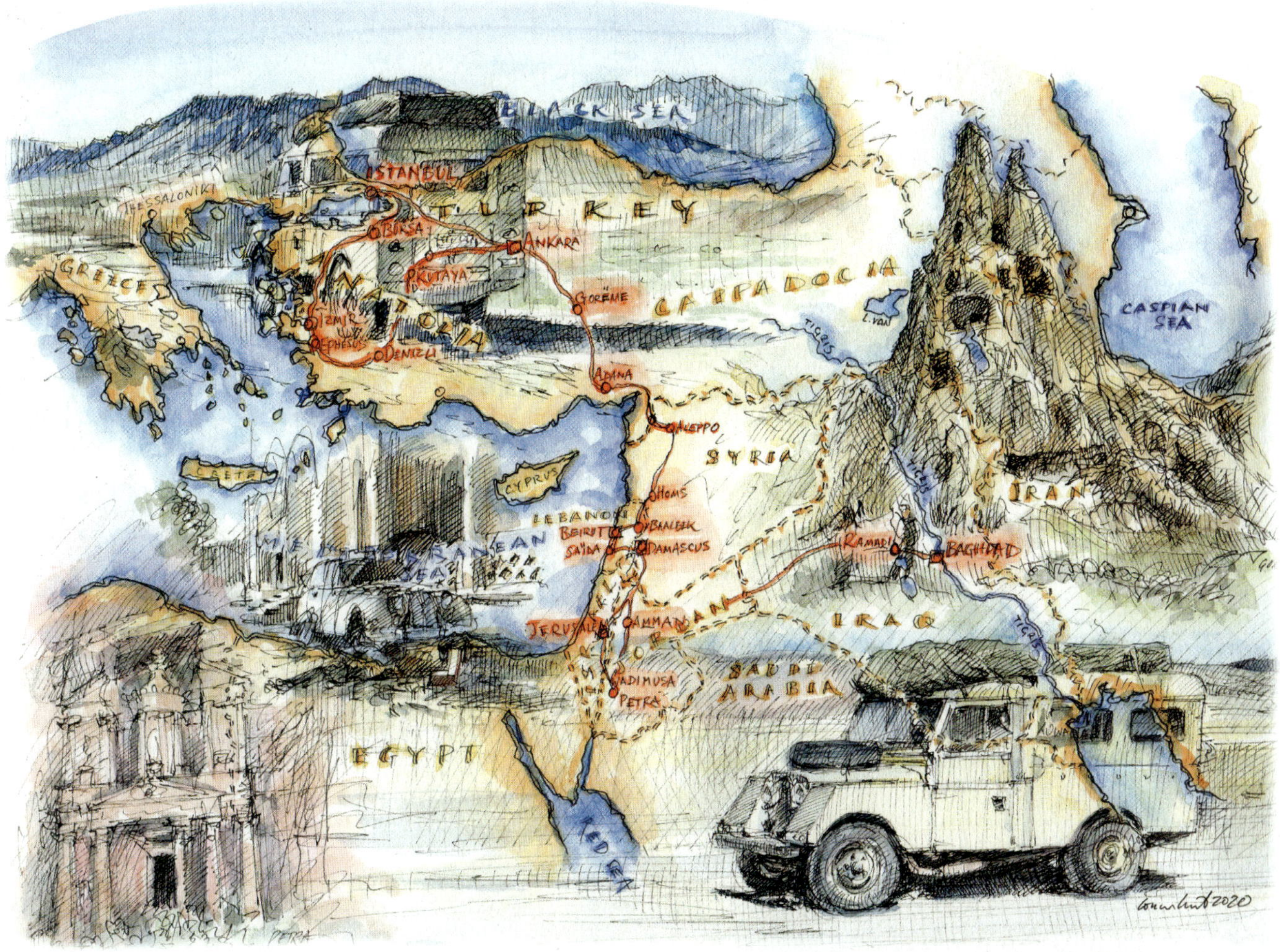

The 107in overturns in Turkey

Damage to the windscreen, roof and front wing

Chevaliers, a Crusader castle near Homs, extensively documenting it for Levie's planned film on Crusader history.

On their way to Lebanon, they were approached by the tribe of the Dambachi family who controlled that area and who showed them the greatest hospitality, enjoying a feast. The leader, with three wives and 18 children, showcased a traditional agricultural lifestyle intertwined with affluence. Late in Beirut, they filmed the cedar forest and Saïda's coastal village, detouring to Baalbek's temple complex.

The full crew reunited in Damascus, exchanging stories and rekindling a lively atmosphere. The Turkey accident with the 107in impacted Levie's filming schedule, reinforcing the importance of vehicle care. The journey progressed to Jordan, with some crew attending a local wedding and assisting the Belgian Consul with a baptism on the banks of the River Jordan, offering insight into local traditions.

Frère ensured the 107in received a service in Amman, where the Land Rover dealer, Mr Malhas, exhibited great hospitality. Despite no issues found during the examination, they tightened the springs and adjusted the steering. The 107in was deemed "good to go," and Frère left the garage impressed with the proprietor's generosity.

A 300km journey from Amman to Wadi Musa, followed by a horseback ride in the mountains, led to Petra. After a night beneath the stars in the desert, they explored the ancient complex, marvelling at the vibrant colours and grand structures. Petra, with its bright orange and red rocks, stood out as the most magical sight of their journey.

After three days of sightseeing in Amman, some of the crew, thanks to Raymond Boschmans' connections, were

Desert tracks in Iran leading from Isfahan

Camel corps patrolling the desert

Nocturnal recording at Persepolis, Iran

Syrian farmers in the valley of Orontes

invited to the palace of 19-year-old King Hussein. The young king showed great interest in the adventures of the Croisière Minerva crew. Meanwhile, Pierre Levie took a side trip to the Dead Sea and the Arabic part of Jerusalem.

The following morning, prepared for a day of filming in Jerusalem and Bethlehem, they discovered a broken rear leaf spring and troubling noises from the rear axle and differential of the 107in. In a rush, gear was loaded into the 80in and the Armstrong Siddeley Sapphire, acting as a makeshift mule. The 107in was taken to the Land Rover dealer in Amman for a proper repair.

Ready for the longest leg of their journey, the vehicles set off for the 900km trek from Amman to Baghdad. Navigating through the volcanic desert landscape, they encountered black basalt rocks flanking the road for hundreds of kilometres. Only two inhabited places, pumping stations H4 and H5, offered refuelling and water.

As the lava belt yielded to the desert, they faced a vast expanse of sand and dunes, and a storm of locusts intensified the feeling of isolation. Formalities at the Iraqi border were swiftly handled, and after refuelling in Ramadi, they crossed the Euphrates River into ancient Mesopotamia. The Tigris River greeted them in the moonlight as they arrived in Baghdad, having covered almost 10,000km.

Contrary to their preconceptions gleaned from folk tales, Baghdad appeared drab and dirty. Paul Frère described it as a city with traffic and little to offer besides some well-preserved monuments. Beggars and servants seeking baksheesh (tips or bribes) added to the weariness of the travellers. Despite this, Sheikh Hassan al Souhail of the Banu Tamim tribe treated them to a lavish banquet at his residence, just outside the city.

During their stay, they detoured to document the Ziggurat of Dur-Kurigalzu, a 14th-century BC brick structure remarkably well-preserved. Exploring the ancient city of Babylon, they filmed the remains of the Ishtar gates, adorned with bas-reliefs of bulls, dragons, and lions. Filmmaker Pierre Levie and his crew travelled north to document the ancient Abbasid Capital of Samarra.

While some enjoyed a rest in Baghdad, Pierre's wife Suzette and son Jean-Pierre flew back to Belgium with the exposed film reels, concluding their part of the adventure after 10,000km on the road. On November 17, 1953, the remaining eight members departed from Baghdad to the Iranian border, joined by a local guide.

Packed into the overloaded Armstrong Siddeley, the Iranian guide, unimpressed with Paul Frère's sportive driving style, opted for another vehicle. Cameraman Philippe Collette, exhausted from driving the 80in Land Rover, chose the comfort of the Armstrong. Battling a torrential downpour on rutted desert tracks towards Tehran, they faced challenges with muddy windscreens, failed dynamo charging and erratic wiper motors, arriving late into the night.

The Iranian capital, Tehran, with its oriental charm, greeted the expedition warmly. Nestled at 1,200m above sea level and surrounded by snow-covered mountains, Tehran's freezing November temperatures did not deter the crew from marvelling at its magnificent setting. The foreign affairs minister welcomed the expedition, and a meeting with the Shah of Iran was scheduled for the next day.

The Shah, a well-educated and affluent ruler, met the Belgians in the garden of his private palace. Eager to learn the details of their adventure, he engaged in lengthy conversations with the crew in impeccable French. They were then treated to a private tour of the usually off-limits Golestan Palace, a magnificent experience.

After covering 10,000km on challenging roads, the vehicles required imminent repairs. The Armstrong Siddeley Frère drove had minor issues with the triangular suspension arms at the front. However, the Boschmans' Sapphire needed more attention, with dented roofs and cracked window pillars.

After welding repairs, the heavy load was redistributed among the other vehicles. The 107in had clutch issues, likely stemming from oil leakage during the previous accident in Turkey. Spare parts were ready, and the dynamo was repaired, ensuring the vehicles were in good shape for the remaining 5,000km. The 80in required minimal maintenance and was ready for the journey ahead.

The road to Isfahan surprised the crew with a newly built, perfectly asphalted road instead of the expected gravel tracks.

Painting 'Ali-baba', the name of Paul Frère's Armstrong, onto its bonnet, Damascus

'Levie utilised his time in New Delhi to review the footage'

Isfahan, the ancient Iranian capital, offered a pleasant cityscape with trees, parks, palaces, and mosques. The film crew documented the city's ancient splendour alongside its modern textile industry. Simultaneously, the rest of the crew secured the necessary filming permits for the upcoming visit to Persepolis.

A unique attraction in Isfahan was the shrine of Monar Jonban, or the Shaking Minarets. The guide demonstrated the shaking of one minaret, causing the other, 10m away, to shake in response. The structural design allowed the movement to transfer through the brick structure, creating a fascinating spectacle.

Heading towards Persepolis, the crew covered 450km, transitioning from asphalt to rocky gravel tracks. Unfortunately, a stone pierced the fuel reservoir of Frère's Sapphire, presenting a challenge in the middle of the desert. With no chewing gum left, they attempted various fixes, but a steady fuel drip persisted. Despite a flat tyre 100km later, they managed to reach Persepolis by evening for repairs.

Persepolis, a ceremonial site built around 550 BC, showcased Darius' grandeur. Although Alexander the Great's invasion in 330 BC caused significant destruction, the large staircase and some frescoes survived. Filming in less than ideal daytime weather, Levie decided to shoot at night, using the 107in lighting set and power generator. Meanwhile, Frère adorned the cars with their itinerary during the nightly hours.

Continuing eastward in late November, the crew faced plummeting temperatures and worsening weather. They had a deadline to meet: Frère and his Armstrong Siddeley Sapphire needed to reach New Delhi by mid-December to board a ship for Italy. Société Nouvelle Minerva's Mathieu Van Roggen had orchestrated this adventure as a publicity stunt, intending to

Isfahan Madrassa, Iran

exhibit the battle-worn car at the Brussels Auto Show in mid January.

Continuing their journey eastward to Yazd on well-maintained tracks, Frère accelerated to around 100km/h in an attempt to catch up with the rest of the crew. However, an unexpected large bump launched the Sapphire into the air, resulting in a violent crash back onto its wheels.

The front wheels were severely misaligned, and the suspension had taken a considerable hit. While field repairs temporarily addressed the steering issue, a garage in the city of Yazd was essential for comprehensive repairs to make the Sapphire roadworthy once again.

After brief stops in the southern Iranian cities of Bam and Zahedan, the crew ventured into the desert toward the border with Pakistan. After covering 50km, the 107in experienced a setback as some of the ➔

Iraq, on the road to Ramadi

Pakistan, having crossed the River Indus

Ruins of the Ziggurat of Dur-Kurigalzu, Baghdad

Pakistan street scene

rear leaf springs broke, unsurprising given the vehicle's continuous overload over the 10,000km journey.

The convoy, always travelling with two vehicles to minimise risks, proceeded slowly to the Jussak border post in the middle of no man's land. Greeted by a foreign ministry attaché who had been anticipating their arrival for two days, the crew underwent the necessary unloading, paperwork and stamping, taking three additional hours. Navigating through the desert at night, they headed towards the next town of Dalbandin, 180km away.

In Dalbandin, the local governor extended an invitation to stay at the 'rest house.' The crew shared accommodations with a young Danish couple who had undertaken a remarkable journey from Denmark to Calcutta on two Vespa scooters. Short on funds for the return journey, they had sold one Vespa and were now sharing a single scooter on their way back to Denmark.

Upon reaching Quetta, the group had to part ways. Frère proceeded to India via the challenging mountain pass towards Multan, a 500km journey involving winding gravel

'The journey had been the adventure of a lifetime'

roads, some of which had to be negotiated in darkness. Driving alone through the night, flanked by towering boulders illuminated by the car's headlights, Frère switched on the miraculously surviving car radio and savoured the moment.

Levie and the remaining crew followed the same road the next day, arriving at the river Indus in the afternoon. Crossing the river was facilitated by a makeshift bridge composed of hundreds of barges linked together and covered with large wooden boards. Regulated by a wooden sign, traffic had to wait for camel convoys to clear the bridge before the Land Rovers and the Sapphire could make the crossing.

The final leg of the journey to New Delhi unfolded without major issues. However, numerous arrangements for the return journey and a planned excursion to Agra, home of the Taj

Mahal, awaited the crew in the city.

Levie utilised his time in New Delhi to review the footage he had captured during the trip. He intended to produce documentaries on the various subjects they'd encountered, including the Crusader Castles, ancient civilisations in Iraq's marshlands and the captivating experiences in India. A new expedition was already in the planning stages for 1956.

Frère boarded the ocean liner MS Victoria bound for Naples with his Sapphire on December 9, 1953. The ten days at sea with excellent weather allowed him to compile the book he had committed to publish. Upon reaching Italy and making a brief stopover in Rome, he drove back to deliver the Sapphire to the Minerva factory in Mortsel.

The journey had been the adventure of a lifetime, fostering camaraderie among the crew that would endure as lifelong friendships. The annual Brussels Motor Show in 1954 held particular significance for Mathieu Van Roggen and Société Nouvelle Minerva.

Having completed a contract for 9,000 80in Minervas for the Belgian Army, Van Roggen aimed to diversify the company's product portfolio. Assembly of the 86in was underway in Mortsel, alongside the local production of Armstrong Siddeley Sapphires. Additionally, development had commenced on a 100% locally designed 4x4, to be launched a year later.

The 107in was repatriated to Belgium, where Pierre Levie later shipped it to the Belgian Congo from Antwerp to assist in subsequent expeditions in Africa in 1956. The film crew extensively documented the local tribes, culture, schools, and industry throughout the country, but the subsequent fate of the reliable 107in remains unknown. **CLR**

n the Land Rover community, we associate trayback trucks with the continent of Australia where they are a popular modification. This is the land which coined the abbreviation 'ute' to describe functional utility vehicles where practicality is of the utmost importance in a challenging environment.

Virtually any truck-cabbed vehicle can be traybacked where any rear tub/bodywork is replaced by a rectangular steel frame and usually a timber-planked decked surface.

More often than not there will be no sides or tailgate. This provides a greater surface area for loads than a pick-up bed. It also raises the load area well above the wheels so no wheel arches interrupt the loading area.

It is much easier to stack boxes onto a trayback and it is easier to strap down a load securely. It is also possible to carry large awkwardly shaped cargo which may be allowed to 'hang out' over the sideless load bed and longer cargo such as timber and plasterboard can be accommodated.

The trayback allows easy access on three sides for loading and access to equipment. Loads of sand and gravel can be easily shovelled off. Many other things could be carried such as water pumps quad bikes or whatever needs shifting.

Of course, a flatbed is ideal for forklift loading and unloading of palleted cargo.

Some traybacks may be equipped with hinged drop sides and tailgates to contain certain loads safely and some may even have hydraulic tipper beds.

The ease of tying down a load securely is important when long journeys over rough corrugated tracks are undertaken while a timber load bed is forgiving, grippy and repairable.

The higher load bed on a trayback also allowed a spare wheel to be mounted under the deck along with cubby boxes for tools and recovery equipment, thus leaving the load bed clear.

When Land Rover exported the 80in very early on they did send complete vehicles but this was soon replaced by what is known as complete knockdown (CKD) kits.

This was down to a variety of reasons some of which were due to taxation and tariffs in the importing country. Regulations existed whereby there had to be a certain amount of 'local' construction in the final vehicle, even if this was only tyres and batteries.

Jacks
of all trades

The trayback is one of the most versatile of Land Rover modifications. **Garry Stuart** takes a closer look at four of them

WORDS AND PICTURES **GARRY STUART**

What's the collective noun?
A truckle of traybacks maybe

Perhaps the assembling companies offered an option to fit a trayback which would have counted as local content but no doubt many were modified later on by farmers and contractors.

In off-road motorsports such as winch challenge, the trayback design has become popular as it provides solutions to the needs of extreme competition. It is weight-saving and provides maximum axle articulation and wheel clearance. It provides an easily accessible load bed for recovery equipment such as tow ropes ground anchors, sledgehammers and hi-lift jacks, all of which need to be securely fastened but remain easy to hand under race/competition conditions.

Here in the UK, there are a growing number of trayback enthusiasts who celebrate this most utility of styles from the early 80ins re-imported from Australia right through to modern Defenders. Check out the Facebook group 'UK Land Rover Trayback Owners' to see the many examples that are roaming free in Britain today.

Peter Wales from Kent will be no stranger to many classic Land Rover enthusiasts as he and his friends organise the annual cross-channel Classic Land Rover Charity Run to different locations in Northern France and Belgium.

It was Peter who created the Facebook Trayback page to bring together fellow enthusiasts whvwere they can show their various interpretations of the trayback theme.

For our CLR photoshoot, Peter roped in another three southeast-based trayback friends and we met up on a farm near Maidstone in Kent.

'Virtually any truck-cabbed vehicle can be traybacked'

A four-strong convoy of 109in traybacks is a rare, possibly unique, sight in the UK

Two options of tray bed. The more traditional wooden planks or modern aluminium base

JAKE SOUGH

Of the four examples in this feature, Jake's trayback is the most 'hot rod' looking with its big wheels and handmade snorkel suggesting that it is intended for fun off-road use as much as it is used as a work vehicle for Jake's metalwork business.

Jake bought the truck from Jon Holmes. It is a 1957 109in which was immediately put on trade plates as it was used as a breakdown truck. It was registered for general road use in 1985 – hence the Q plate.

The chassis needed a lot of welding which Jake was able to do himself. A replacement bulkhead came from Australia which only needed a little welding action.

Under the bonnet lies a 300Tdi engine making this a very useable working truck delivering its power through an LT77 gearbox and a 1.2 ratio Discovery transfer box. Jake also converted the original clutch linkage to hydraulic.

The front axle is stock Series One but the rear is a Salisbury unit. The steering is standard Series One, as are the brakes, but the suspension has been uprated to parabolic leaf springs.

Jake fitted it with an aluminium radiator with an electric fan and plumbed it in himself. He also fabricated the snorkel air intake. The fuel tank is a custom aluminium 95-litre unit and the seats were supplied by Undercover Covers.

Jake driving his uprated 109in

Big beadlock wheels and tyres give Jake's truck an aggressive stance

A modified transmission tunnel accommodates an LT77 gearbox

300 Tdi engine conversion makes this an effective work truck for Jake's metalworking business

This truck is kept busy transporting parts for John's Land Rover restoration business

JOHN CHARMAN

John's 109in trayback is a UK vehicle which has only had one previous owner since its registration in 1958. It lived in West Sussex so has spent its whole life in the southeast. When John found the truck it was a sorry collection of bits with a busted chassis and everything needed to be done to get it back on the road. It is therefore fortuitous that John's business is rebuilding Land Rovers so he undertook all of the necessary work which only took him three months to accomplish.

His original intention was to sell it on but he "fell in love with it" so it stayed and became his daily driver alongside his 80in V8.

John decided to build the trayback rear as it

Standard interior with the only luxury, a warm blanket for Milo

The last owner fitted a Rover P4 engine which John says pulls well when towing

John has equipped his truck with an effective anti-theft device, Milo

gave him a lot more space and made loading and transporting awkwardly shaped chassis for project vehicles a whole lot easier.

The previous owner had fitted a Rover P4 engine and this has been retained as it is a good power unit that zips along and has great torque when towing. Apart from that, it is all original.

PETER WALES

Peter has owned 'Bruce' (pronounced in an Aussie accent) since 2018. It is a 1958 109 and it came fitted with an Australian Holden V8 motor. It has since been recommissioned and fettled by Mike Rivett and it is now driven by a 2,286cc Series III five-bearing petrol engine and gearbox.

The trayback rear was bespoke fitted by a company in Victoria Australia called Vawdrey.

Some people have experienced a hitch when registering a CKD vehicle in the UK. The DVLA in some cases did not accept the year of manufacture in Solihull but wanted the paperwork appertaining to the date the CKD vehicle was assembled in Australia. Peter had no issues as he had all of the relevant paperwork.

It is not Peter's intention to use the trayback commercially but rather as a leisure vehicle for local running around and attending classic car shows. No doubt it will not be too long before a friend or family member realises it would be ideal for moving a three-piece suite or suchlike! ➲

A beautifully clean and straight interior

This is a five-bearing Series III engine with shiny new carb and alternator

Bumper plaque is from the annual Classic Land Rover Charity Rally that Peter organises

This trayback rear was bespoke fitted by Vawdrey of Victoria Australia

MIKE RIVETT

Mike puts this truck through its paces at work most days

Three years ago Mike's 1958 109in trayback arrived in the UK after a lifetime spent on an Australian farm. It was sourced by a friend John Spears who located it on a farm close to where Peter Wales' trayback also worked. Close meaning hundreds of miles apart in Aussie terms. It had been abandoned to die but the surge in popularity for these old pioneers ensured a new lease of life here in the UK.

When it arrived Mike confirmed that it was rust-free and required no welding. It was powered by a Holden engine which was knackered so a period-correct two-litre petrol Rover.

Mike has retained the farm-spec 'roo bars' so this truck retains its distinctive Aussie accent leaving no one in any doubt as to its origins.

Mike gave it a squirt of original grey paint which he then distressed, in keeping with the rest of the vehicle.

It is sign-written with the Rivett company name and this little workhorse is used nearly every day.

The seatbacks are original with Exmoor-supplied bases. It came with mix-and-match wheels but now it is running on proper Australian-stamped Series One rims.

The lights are original but Mike fitted a new Autosparks wiring loom. He also restored the whole braking system to original specification.

Because Mike uses his trayback to carry proper loads he replaced and uprated the springs to heavy-duty parabolics. The axles are original stock equipment. Even the glass in the vehicle is original.

Mike loves the fact that the trayback gives him a larger more accessible load area and he also finds that it is a great workbench out in the field of operation. **CLR**

Mike fitted a period-correct two-litre petrol engine

Traybacks are suitable for strapping loads on. A nice personalised old-school petrol can

Australian-stamped Series One wheels with Power Train locking hubs

The original roo bars may deflect the odd Muntjac deer in Kent

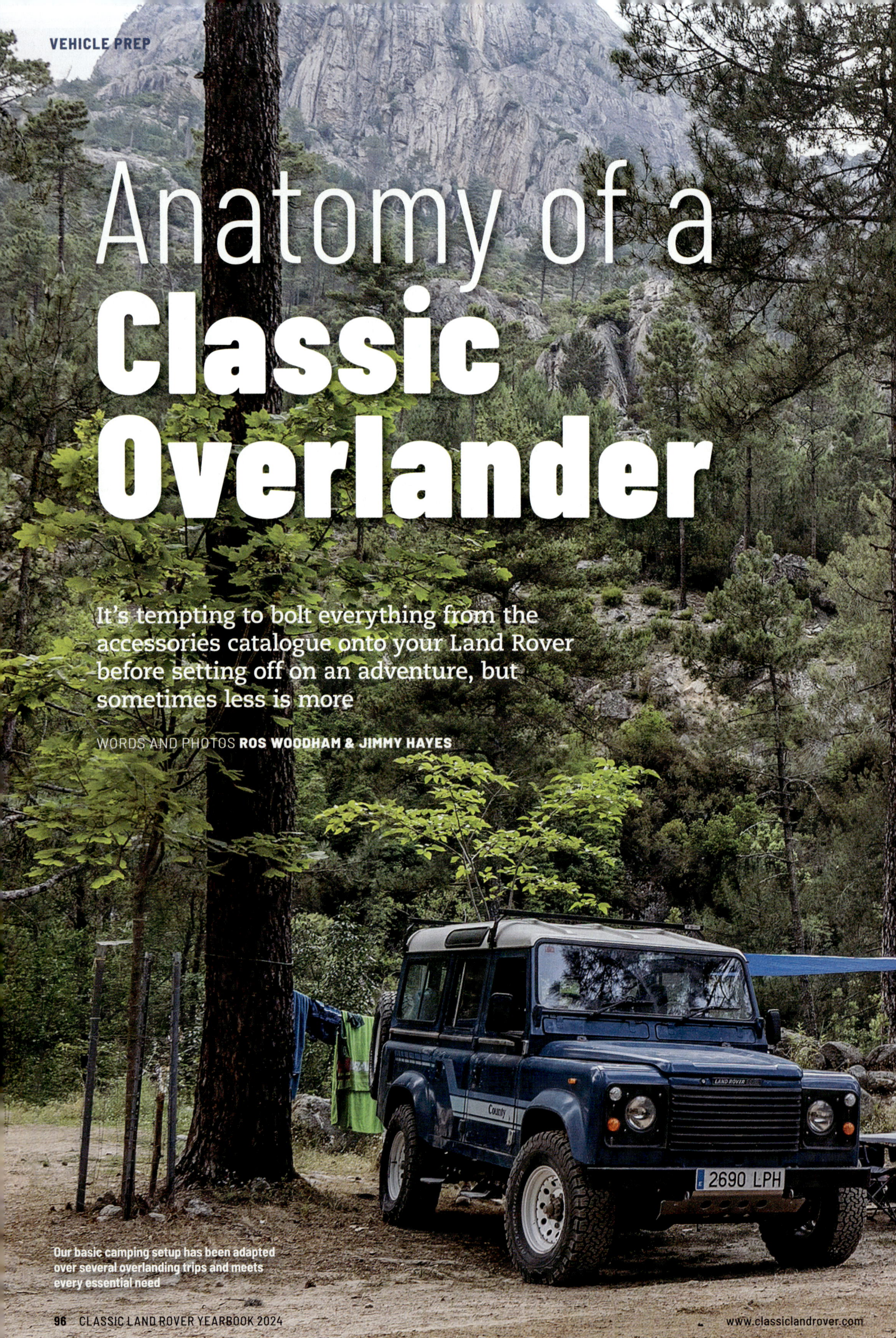

Anatomy of a
Classic Overlander

It's tempting to bolt everything from the accessories catalogue onto your Land Rover before setting off on an adventure, but sometimes less is more

WORDS AND PHOTOS **ROS WOODHAM & JIMMY HAYES**

Our basic camping setup has been adapted over several overlanding trips and meets every essential need

There are lots of things to take into consideration when preparing your vehicle for an overland adventure, such as the duration, number of occupants, types of terrain, climate and distances between 'civilisation'.

Having a full roof rack, for instance, looks the business, but there are other considerations too, like the raised centre of gravity (not ideal on side slopes), and increased fuel consumption.

No two Land Rovers will be equipped the same. Our One Ten, which is primarily used for family holidays around Europe, is a bit light on the accessories front, but as the kids get older and our plans get more ambitious, we do not doubt that the Land Rover will be adapted accordingly.

TYRES

Tyres are a primary consideration when equipping any vehicle for overland adventure. After all, it is the tyres which keep the vehicle in contact with the road, so investing in a quality set of rubber will be money well spent. BFG All-Terrains have always been our tyre of choice. In the 17 years that we have been running BFG tyres, we have never yet had a puncture or a problem (jinx!).

STORAGE

A place for everything and everything in its place? Not usually, but having a good storage system helps to keep gear separated and organised. We bought cargo cages and a load shelf from Flatdog UK which transformed the load space of the Land Rover and made everything easily accessible. We also built a crude but very useful false floor in the load area. This not only added another shelf for stacking and organising, but it also created a 'secret' space, right at the back and out of sight, where we could store valuables when leaving the truck unattended.

Occupants with single-figure ages usually have their own ideas about what gear is

Cargo cages, a storage rack and a false floor keep the load space organised

A windbreak for the stove has been one of our best buys. Scrambled eggs in any weather!

'essential', so we also removed the second-row middle seat and installed a cubby box in its place so that the kids could stash their own things and have something to lean on.

FRIDGE

We used to think that a fridge was a luxury item before we finally bought one. Having had one for the last two years we consider this a 'must-have' for any overland trip, especially in warmer climates. There are not many home comforts when overlanding

Mounting the potentially explosive gas bottle outside the vehicle is sensible

in an old truck, so being able to have cold milk with your breakfast or a cold beer at the end of a long day is a welcome treat. Additionally, as well as reducing the need to buy fresh supplies daily, there are other important considerations, like being able to keep medicine refrigerated, as we found out on our recent trip to Corsica.

SPLIT CHARGE SYSTEM

If you are going to run a fridge then you will need to install a leisure battery to avoid depleting your starter battery. In our One Ten, a second battery was fitted beside the first with a simple split charge system, keeping the fridge running when the engine is switched off.

POWER

A family of four has an assortment of electronic devices to keep charged, from cameras, phones and iPads to portable lamps and laptops. Our split charge system allows us to use the USB sockets at any time. However, we don't want to be stuck inside the cab when using a device that is being charged, so we recently bought a

A simple tarp with extendable poles, mounted to the roof bars creates a very affordable and easy-to-use awning

battery-powered inverter generator from Jackary which we now couldn't do without. It can be charged from the USB socket on the move and later used anywhere around the camp for charging multiple devices.

AWNING

Whether it's shade from the burning sun or shelter from the rain, you'll most likely need some respite from the elements, even more so if you're travelling with kids and plan to do a lot of camping. An awning attached to the side of the vehicle is the obvious choice. There are a lot of different awnings on the market for various budgets, but you don't have to re-mortgage the house; our 'homemade' version cost a grand total of £80 for the tarp and poles and works a treat. If you don't want to fit roof bars like us, the tarp can also be attached using heavy-duty suction cups!

RECOVERY EQUIPMENT

Our experience overlanding has taught us to avoid getting into sticky situations unnecessarily, but sometimes it isn't possible to just 'go around'. Getting stuck isn't the end of the world, but it helps if you can get unstuck without too much difficulty. Having solid and accessible recovery points is a no-brainer; good straps and properly rated shackles are also a must.

CAMPING GEAR

There's no need to 'rough it' just because you are camping. Our Exped Deep Sleep

insulated mattresses and down-filled sleeping bags ensure sleeping comfort just like home. Overlanding can be physically and mentally demanding so a good night's sleep is essential for endurance and stamina. We believe that a tent, however, is less important and we usually pack our lightweight family tent for ease and speed.

Cooking up a decent meal at the end of the day is an enjoyable part of overlanding so be sure to bring a comprehensive set of cooking equipment and utensils. Multi-use items like sporks and mess tins can save on space, weight and washing up!

LIGHTING

There's nothing worse than bad lighting when the daylight dwindles. A decent head torch (with spare batteries) and some portable lamps – perhaps rechargeable or solar-powered – for ambient light around the camp are a must.

SAFETY

If gas is your fuel of choice, a heavy gas bottle stored inside the vehicle is a potential projectile in the event of a collision, so we opted for a dedicated bottle holder mounted to the back of the vehicle.

It's also important to carry the correct fire safety equipment such as a fire extinguisher which should be checked regularly.

Lastly, a comprehensive first-aid kit and knowledge of how and where to get emergency help are essential at all times. **CLR**

Leisure battery fits snugly beside the starter battery under the passenger seat

The split-charge system manages the two batteries allowing us to run the fridge overnight

---

OUR ESSENTIAL GEAR LIST

Accessories:
- Roof bars (to fit awning)
- Gas bottle holder
- Cargo cages + load shelf
- Leisure battery + split charge system
- Basic underbody protection
- Recovery points
- Awning
- Relevant spares + tools
- Fridge

Kit:
- Recovery straps + shackles
- Shovel
- Hi-lift jack
- Compressor
- Tyre deflator
- Quality storage boxes
- Cooking stove
- Cooking utensils
- Portable power bank (such as Jackary)
- Tent
- Bedding that ensures a good sleep
- Good-sized table
- Chairs for everyone
- Head torches
- Portable lamps/lanterns
- Fire extinguisher
- First aid kit
- Breakdown kit (hi-vis, warning triangles etc.
- Hand-held CBs for communication

Dedicated recovery points are essential

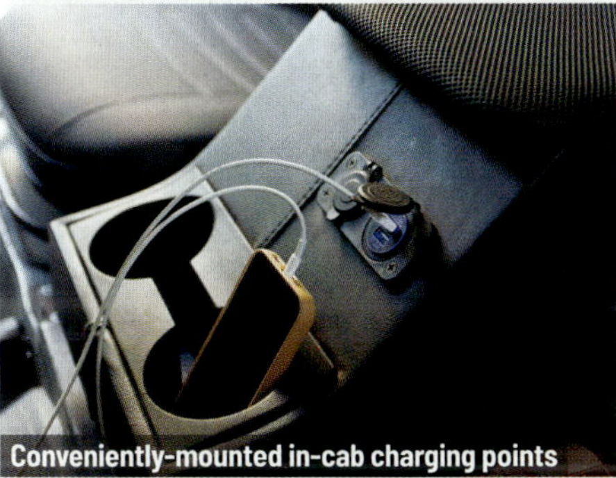
Conveniently-mounted in-cab charging points

> 'We used to think that a fridge was a luxury item before we finally bought one'

Just some of the gear we pack for any overlanding trip, regardless of duration

EURO ADVENTURE

Carla Binder and Jamie Cook visit
five countries in three weeks in their
1969 Series IIA fire engine

WORDS AND PICTURES **CARLA BINDER**   ILLUSTRATION **LOUISE LIMB**

When my partner Jamie Cook still owned his Series III 88in, he planned a massive adventure in it. However, whenever he drove it for just 30 miles, people laughed, let alone 1,800 miles. So, when we met, we both had the same goal: to prove people wrong while undertaking an adventure we had both always dreamed of.

Jamie sold his Series III, but together we bought Finley, a 1969 Series IIA fire engine which we planned to use on the adventure. We then set about converting it into a camper, which you can read more about in the July 2023 issue of CLR.

Once we had made up our minds to go, it was my job to plan the details of the journey while Jamie focused on getting Finley ready for the trip.

Jamie drove Finley to work daily for at least a month or more to ensure it was ready. But the night before we were due to set off there was a last-minute rush as the brakes started playing up.

The master cylinder and two front wheel cylinders had sprung leaks, so with help from Jamie's dad, Michael, we were hard at work trying to get Finley ready for an early morning start.

I also had to drive late at night to a friend's

house to borrow an ignition because Finley's decided not to work at the last minute (still borrowing it, sorry, Jeff).

We got things sorted just hours before we were due to leave and eventually set off on a three-week road trip around Europe covering France, Belgium, the Netherlands, Germany, the Czech border, and Luxembourg.

The trip would be the furthest we had covered in the vehicle since buying it and we were well prepared with around 80% of our storage filled with parts as we know how unpredictable Land Rovers can be.

After crossing the Channel, we 'officially'

A sunflower field in Germany

started our road trip in Calais, France and headed for Belgium and our first stop – a town called Verne. It rained for most of the drive and the following day we drove to Ypres, going through the Menin Gate and seeing the famous Last Post at sunset.

We also called in at Tyne Cot cemetery, where we met a group riding Lambrettas and some Yorkshire bikers. They were going to the same campsite as us and from there we kept on bumping into them as our trip progressed.

As we were about to leave, they handed us two tins of cassoulet which wasn't the best-tasting thing in the world, but as they

'The warm weather beginning to take its toll on Finley'

said, when you are hungry, it doesn't matter.

The next stop was Valkenswaard in the Netherlands, which was the beginning of the Operation Market Garden route. This is where we found one of our favourite campsites – it even had an on-site cheese shop. What's not to love?

The following day we travelled to Nijmegen where we found a secluded

spot along the River Waal. There was no one else apart from another caravan, but with plenty of room, we barely knew they were there. There was a small beach and watching the sunset go down while cooking dinner was amazing.

As our journey progressed, the one thing we both enjoyed was having our belongings in one place and the flexibility to change the route whenever we wanted.

For the second stage of our journey, we crossed the border into Germany and drove to a small town outside Cologne.

The most interesting part was driving along the Autobahn at 45km/h and seeing ➔

everybody else, including lorries and coaches, overtaking us (apart from a couple of Trabants we encountered).

While en route to Colditz Castle, we stopped at a beautiful campsite outside Paderborn boasting magnificent views. The campsite was owned by an elderly gentleman but run by his granddaughter.

There was a collection of tractors and, surprisingly, two fire engines, which spanned 15 different barns.

Of course, he took a keen interest in Finley. He said the reason he owned two fire engines was because the nearest fire station was two hours away, so he decided to buy some in case they were needed.

While we were mostly lucky with campsites, just a word of caution if you use online resources to find them. Some may look amazing in the daytime, but at night it could be another story. For example, despite finding a site offering incredible views in the middle of Germany, we were

Finley pictured with a Series Land Rover belonging to a couple in Rabenstein

Colditz Castle

Jamie concentrating while on the way to Colditz

warned it was a 'dodgy' area and had to hide Finley between a row of hedges.

With our trip going well we made good time and on the 10th day arrived at Colditz Castle near the Czech border. We were able to stay in the castle that night, which was a fantastic experience as it's not like you get to say you've stayed in Colditz Castle every day!

We looked around the rooms and towers and were able to view the famous replica glider similar to the one built by prisoners during World War Two.

With the rain forecast, we decided Colditz Castle would be our turning point for the long drive home. Leaving Colditz the following day, we headed for a farm that felt

Camping along the River
Waal, Nijmegen

Last minute fixes the day before we left

Rothenburg ob der Tauber

'It's not like you get to say you've stayed in Colditz Castle every day'

When they bought their Land Rover they had no idea what they had and struggled to get parts, but now a restoration is on the go and Jamie is still in contact with them.

We made our way to Rothenberg, which is a fairytale-like town in northern Bavaria known for its medieval architecture. As soon as you go through the town's gates you are met with multicoloured houses and it feels like you have stepped into a film set from Chitty Chitty Bang Bang. The campsite we stayed at was nearby, so we visited in the evening when it was much quieter and this was one of my favourite places.

With summer temperatures rising we drove to Heidelberg, the warm weather beginning to take its toll on Finley. I'm not sure who felt the heat more, us or the Land Rover, and we had never been so relieved to walk into a supermarket with air conditioning.

We found a campsite along a lovely river, the unfortunate part being it was one of those places where you just pitched your tent or motorhome 'wherever'. Unfortunately, when we returned from our travels around the city centre, we had a VW Td5 parked so close to us that we couldn't open the back

like it was in the middle of nowhere.

We were the only ones staying there and we had to use the farmhouse for the bathroom. We were there at the time the women's European final football match was being played between England and Germany and when England won we celebrated loudly.

Our favourite story from the trip, though, was meeting a German couple in Rabenstein near Chemnitz. While I went to pay for a night's stay at the campsite, Jamie got 'talking' to them but they spoke very little English. As we spoke very little German there was plenty of miming and gesticulating with our hands. We were eventually shown a Series II Land Rover.

It was a real surprise to see the vehicle in what felt like the middle of nowhere in Germany. With a few goes at Google translate, we discovered this was the first time the couple had seen another Land Rover.

River Moselle, Bernkastel-Kues

door to get in. So, we asked our next-door neighbours in a caravan if we could park closer to them and, thanks to a bit more miming, were able to move.

The next day will never be forgotten. While on our way to the start of the River Moselle in Koblenz, we had an overheating issue with Finley (later found to be a piece of silicone in the radiator). The air temperature was 37° and driving up hills didn't help.

A journey that was supposed to take two hours turned into seven gruelling hours with the heating on to cool down the engine. We had to stop on every hill we climbed due to overheating.

This resulted in a rethinking of our route and we found a valley to drive through which followed the River Rhine to the beginning of the River Moselle, which was fantastic to see.

The scenery was amazing, but I probably would have appreciated it more if not for worrying about Finley so much.

For the next three days, we followed the River Moselle with the bright red Land Rover attracting plenty of interest from tourists taking photos.

At one point we hiked up the side of a cliff and once we got up to the top, it was breathtaking. Well, we thought we were at the top but then realised that to get to the actual top, you had to do some rock climbing so I looked after the wine while Jamie climbed to the top and took lots of photos.

We stayed in a fancy hotel on the last day of our trip along the river. We saw Lamborghinis, Ferraris and many other sports cars arriving at the hotel. And then there was poor old Finley, who hadn't been washed in nearly three weeks. The most amusing thing was that Finley couldn't fit in the underground car park, so had to be parked outside the front for the night.

The next day we departed early as we needed to cross three countries in a day; completing the remainder of our trip in Germany before entering Luxembourg and then crossing into Belgium.

Once in Belgium, we drove through the

'A journey that was supposed to take two hours turned into seven gruelling hours'

Ardennes to Bastogne where we went to the Bastogne War Museum. It's worth a visit and that night we stayed near to the 101st Airborne foxholes. They were from the Easy Company of the 101st Airborne Division in World War Two and are well preserved and maintained. It was an eye-opening experience to see them and you can only imagine what it must have been like for soldiers at the time.

The following day we headed for Dinant, a city in Belgium's Walloon region, where we got stopped quite a few times by people wanting to look at and comment on Finley.

Before heading to Calais, we returned to Ypres where we celebrated a successful journey. Despite the overheating issues, we'd not had any breakdowns and had only needed one cambelt change.

Finley had 'drunk' plenty of oil and petrol, but overall it wasn't too bad for a nearly 2,000-mile round trip in a 54-year-old Series Land Rover.

Sure, we could have done it in a newer model vehicle, but would it have been as much fun not having to concentrate on steering, double clutching, and driving at a max speed of 50mph (downhill)? I think not, and this is why it was such an adventure for us and one we will never forget. **CLR**

The last morning on our road trip underneath the Menin Gate

DISCO

The Discovery HC blends exclusivity with classic appeal according to its marketers HC Classics

MANIA

From whichever angle you look at it, the Discovery HC is an impressive vehicle, but is the world ready for a £100,000 Discovery? Richard Carp of HC Classics thinks so

WORDS **ANDREW STONE**
PICTURES **ANDREW STONE, HC CLASSICS**

It was bound to happen. After years of Land Rover Defenders being re-engineered into high-end custom classics appealing to buyers with deep pockets, a UK-based company has reimagined the Discovery 1 along similar lines.

HC Classics outside Salisbury in Wiltshire has turned everyone's family-favourite Land Rover into an exclusive classic that is ready for adventure.

Featuring bespoke leather interiors with carbon fibre inserts, a galvanised chassis, specially engineered front and rear bumpers, air suspension and a camping kit list that would impress Bear Grylls, the Discovery HC has undergone a complete body-off restoration with a reconditioned engine. So, it's not only a tough and capable off-roader but can serve as an everyday family car too.

Whether you want to tow your horsebox down a country lane or take the family away on a weekend adventure in style and comfort, this could be the vehicle for you. There's just one important consideration: style, comfort and what is essentially an entirely 'new' car come at a price – just short of £100,000 to be precise.

So, is the world ready for this new era of Discovery ownership? HC Classics director and long-time Land Rover enthusiast Richard Carp believes so. "What we've created is an exclusive vehicle with classic appeal," explained Richard. "We've seen how prices have risen for Series Land Rovers and Defenders over the years and I think the same is going to happen with the Discovery. It's already happening. It's a comfortable vehicle, has great vision, is a stylish looking car, yet it has got all the practicalities of any other Land Rover."

HC Classics is not the only company to get in early on these types of Discovery conversions with Revel Machines in the US doing something similar to Discovery 1s and 2s. "We started with the idea of creating a serious off-road car but reconsidered and took it back to a road car and that is how the project has developed," said Richard.

"People who want to do serious off-roading don't want to spend a lot of money. Our Discovery is a great lifestyle vehicle aimed at owners who want something unique that they can take on weekend adventures with their family and friends, go fishing with or even take overlanding to Morocco if they wanted."

Having started in 2017, HC Classics has since grown from an automotive upholstery business into a full-blown classic car restoration company with workshops in the UK and Poland.

Richard, an automotive designer working mainly on interiors, used to be based in Germany where he was employed by a company that made the instrumentation and interiors for the main German marques – Audi, Mercedes-Benz, BMW and Porsche. "We also did work for Swedish companies, SAAB and Volvo," he said. "I then joined another design company based in Letchworth and essentially they worked on everything that moved, be it wheels or wings.

"I have always been a classic car fan and have always had my own classics. I needed some trimming done and couldn't find an upholsterer local to me who could do the work efficiently and in good time, so I realised there was a gap in the market.

"I believe in luck and was very lucky one day when I visited a local classic car company that said they were also looking for an upholsterer. So, I had a client right on my doorstep. We built a workshop, found upholsterers to employ and just got going. We've grown from initially employing two upholsterers to start with and now have five and a mechanic."

Richard said that as a small business, they had initially developed a niche and reputation for the quality of their work on Bristol motor vehicles. "From Bristols we branched out to AC Cobras

'You recognise it as a Discovery, but you know it's not like any Discovery you've ever seen'

and classic Aston Martins and Peugeots. We're very lucky in that we have developed a good client base thanks to the quality of our work.

"We moved from just doing upholstery into restorations through demand from our clients who want a one-stop shop. They don't want to go to different suppliers and negotiate with them. So, in 2019 we got our first restoration project, a 1950 Bristol 401. It was a very successful project for us on the basis that we turned around the entire project within 18 months including the interior."

Having always had a passion for Land Rovers, Richard has through the years owned a V8 County Station Wagon in the mid-1980s, a three-door Discovery 1 "which was a great car", a Range Rover Vogue "which I absolutely loved", and a

Discovery 2 from new, "which was not as good as the Discovery 1".

"It had enormous gearbox problems and non-stop oil leaks from new and I eventually bailed out after about three months," he explained. "I now have a 1973 Bahama Gold three-door Classic Range Rover and I do like it. The original Range Rover to me is the absolute epitome of 4x4s. It's the shape to die for and everyone else has followed it. It is the most beautiful car and every time I wheel it out, even people who don't know about cars, admire it."

Richard is not the company's only Land Rover enthusiast though, with several employees led by workshop general manager, Ilja Szklinski, also fans of the brand. "We live close to the A303 and at weekends see people going down to the west country in their campers and Land

Rovers, so we thought we need to corner that market," said Richard.

"The idea was further accelerated by the staycation drive due to Covid as people stopped travelling abroad and stayed in the country. This is why we decided to add on a lot more kit to the Discovery HC to offer the

With the optional, self-opening roof top

While instantly recognisable, the Discovery HC is unique in many respects

HC Classics director Richard Carp has long been a Land Rover enthusiast

The quality of finishes is superb

The base vehicles are completely stripped down and rebuilt ensuring a high-quality finish

All-terrain tyres have been fitted

Side steps come as standard

opportunity to go camping."

Richard said they had settled on the Discovery and not the Defender as it is a lot more refined and comfortable than the latter vehicle and "you can see out of it a lot better".

"We've never been concerned about the resale value of the Discovery," he said. "We're early to the market while everyone else has been doing Defenders and we wanted to do something different.

"I liked having Discoverys, apart from the one that leaked oil. It's a great vehicle and one I believe is very underrated. You see individuals doing restorations with them, but not companies like us, so we wanted to set the trend."

The Discovery 1 ES model is used as the base vehicle for the HC as it comes standard with air conditioning, electric seats, and is automatic. "The aircon is essential as you don't want to retrofit that," said Richard. "What we're hoping to do is offer a 300Tdi, V8 and a full electric conversion."

HC Classics has seven vehicles in stock at present including a V8 and a demo model. "If a client was to place an order today, I would go through a shopping list with them," explained Richard.

"We have standard equipment and then optional gear and discuss what the customer wants. We then take the base car and completely transform it into what is effectively a 'new' car from top to bottom.

"They are completely stripped down for a full body-off restoration starting

'It's a great vehicle and one I believe is very underrated'

with a galvanised chassis. The Discovery bodies were known for rotting, particularly around the rear wheel arches and floors and everything will be replaced and treated. Customers can choose whatever they want, from the colour of the interior to the body colour – it's all flexible and is designed to be exclusive. But I can't emphasise enough that these are built as new.

"In the end, the car has got to be guaranteed to work and we stick to that ethos in terms of what we do. You're guaranteed to have something bespoke and tailored to your needs and tastes, so it is for someone who wants something slightly different but still offers the attractions of an authentic Discovery experience of adventure and family motoring."

Prices for the Discovery HC start at £99,750 with standard equipment and increase depending on the level of optional equipment and type of drivetrain wanted.

"If you want the all-electric version it'll cost another £60,000," said Richard. "Considering it's such a bespoke order, our turnaround time is good – about nine months from the date of order. It takes about six months to build the car and three months to put the interior in."

A 12-month parts and labour warranty is included in the price.

Sitting in the Discovery HC is a strange experience. You recognise it as a Discovery, but you know it's not like any Discovery you've ever seen. The finely crafted leather interior is complemented by a big-screen Alpine infotainment system and carbon fibre inserts have been placed at strategic points.

The seats are standard but have been reupholstered and new Dynamat soundproofing has been fitted throughout. Cranked radius arms have been added to raise the suspension slightly, which has been completely upgraded and also features stiffer springs.

"Air suspension has been fitted as standard to adjust the ride," said Richard. "Early Discoverys were quite wallowy and we're trying to stop that while retaining a level of comfort."

Standard specification includes items such as front and rear LED light conversions, a dual battery system, a winch, a compressed air pump, a safe for valuables, a 240V inverter, roller drawers in the rear, a roof rack and water and fuel containers.

"We get that it's a lot of money for a Discovery, but we're not talking about producing big numbers and our quality and exclusivity means you get a vehicle that's tailor-made for you and unique," said Richard.

"We've thought about all the details and along with our optional list of equipment the vehicle wants for nothing." **CLR**

IN THE FOOTSTEPS OF
ALEXANDER THE GREAT

Nearly 30 years ago, Toby Savage borrowed a new Range Rover 2.5 Diesel to complete an 8,000-mile run to the Syrian border and back

WORDS AND PICTURES **TOBY SAVAGE**

I have always liked to link my travel to some historical event or person, retracing the routes of various past heroes. Back in 1995, as a young and ambitious adventurer, I started studying the impressive life of Alexander the Great. Just the title added enormous gravitas!

I can't imagine any of today's world leaders being known as 'the Great'. Alexander inherited the Macedonian throne from his father Philip II in 336 BC at the age of 20 and spent most of his ruling years conducting a lengthy military campaign throughout Western Asia and Egypt.

By the age of 30, he had created one of the largest empires in history, stretching from Greece to northwestern India. Even more impressive is that he achieved all of this before his premature death in Babylon, at the age of 32.

Throughout his reign, he had just one horse named Bucephalus and I thought I needed my own Bucephalus to complete a journey in Alexander's footsteps. A rough calculation showed that my Bucephalus and I could probably get to the southern border of Turkey, where it meets Syria within a three-week break. This would allow me time to visit many of the sites in Turkey that secured Alexander's rule in Asia Minor.

The P38 Range Rover had recently been

Everyday street-scenes in Antakya, a city that would be devastated by the earthquakes of 2022

'My plan was nearly ruined at the border into Bulgaria as my visa had expired'

launched and I had driven one at the press launch and was impressed. The press officer, Colin Walkey had hinted to me that if I had an interesting trip coming up, I could borrow one. I put in a successful request for the BMW-engined 2.5 diesel and my adventure was secured.

I plotted a route that would take me southeast through Germany, Austria, Hungary and Serbia to Alexander's birthplace, Pella in Macedonia. The new Range Rover went well, being able to maintain a fast motorway cruising speed, yet returning a reasonable fuel consumption.

The comfort levels were high and the excellent ride-on airbags and high seating position allowed for stress-free motoring.

I was able to cover vast distances with minimal breaks and reach my destinations ahead of schedule.

Once in Pella, it was a privilege to wander around the ruins of the old palace and have the place to myself. It was easy to imagine a young Alexander growing up there, where he was educated by Aristotle.

I then continued east, as Alexander had done, towards Turkey, crossing the border at Ipsala. From there I went south through the Gallipoli peninsula. This was a very special place to me, as my grandfather had fought there in World War One.

I drove onto the sand at Sulva Bay where he had landed as a young captain in the winter of 1915 and looked up the steep

One of many scenes found in rural Turkey, little changed over the centuries and people were happy to be photographed

thorn-covered hill that formed such an effective barrier protecting the German and Turkish troops at the top. Little wonder that so many lives were lost and it was regarded as a military failure.

I then took a small ferry from Kilitbahir to Çanakkale. The same crossing that Alexander had made in 334 BC. From there I headed directly south visiting the ruins of many of his conquests; Sardis, Miletus and Halicarnassos and, while in the region, the Roman Theatre of Ephesus, near Selçuk.

Entry to all of these important historical sights was either free or very cheap. In 1995 the rate of exchange between the UK pound and the Turkish lire was very favourable, making most things half the cost of at home.

My personal Bucephalus was proving to be the perfect steed for the journey, as some locations were only accessible

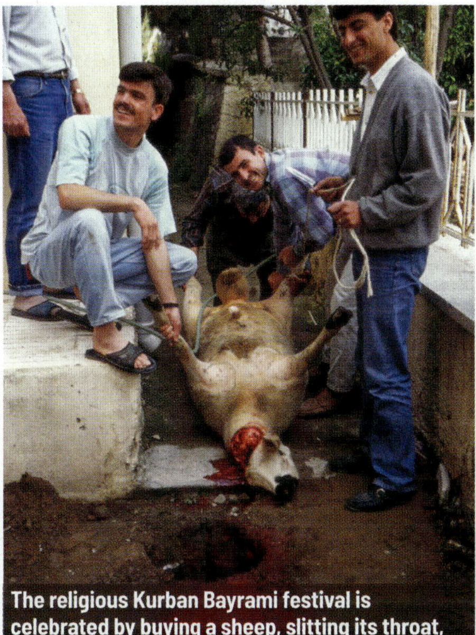

The religious Kurban Bayrami festival is celebrated by buying a sheep, slitting its throat, then eating it as part of a feast

The town of Afyon is dominated by this rock outcrop. During World War One British prisoners of war who had been captured at Gallipoli were housed here in an empty church at the foot of the rock

Lake Burdur in central Turkey. Miles of flat salt lake to drive on

by track and recent rain had made them muddy. It was at Sardis that I managed to get stuck in some deep ruts. I felt rather foolish with all four wheels spinning and the floor of the car bottomed out.

I was quite a long way up the track and there was nobody about. This could have been a real problem, but after about half an hour a tractor passed and I engaged in a conversation using only sign language to indicate I was stuck and needed help.

The farmer produced a length of rope and we tied it between the two vehicles. He had clearly done this sort of thing before as he gently pulled me free of the mud. I rewarded him with a generous tip and continued my journey with a mud-splattered Range Rover.

There followed a very scenic run ➲

Minding his flock. This Turkish shepherd wears the traditional felt cape to keep the wind out

Just one of thousands of houses cut into the rocks in Cappadocia

'I was able to cover vast distances with minimal breaks'

along the coast road with views of the Mediterranean to my right and the mountains to my left. Alexander must have taken the same route before heading north to Termessos, one of very few locations he did not capture, due to its location.

As I drove the Range Rover up its steep access roads I could understand why. Even a small population could frustrate an attacking army with such a high location. My climb was rewarded by the enjoyment of sitting in the empty amphitheatre at the top with commanding views across the Taurus Mountains.

I was now heading inland and away from the busy coastline and it was like winding the clock back 100 years. There were farmers with donkey carts, shepherds in traditional dress and very few cars. I took some tracks that seemed to go roughly in the right direction and arrived late in the afternoon on the shores of Lake Burdur, a natural salt lake.

As it was getting late, I drove into the nearby town of Isparta, where my Rough Guide informed me there was a cheap guesthouse described as 'eccentric'! I found it and checked in for the night, enjoying the eccentricity of the flamboyant owner and his parrot, the creaking staircase with a step missing, and the low doorway that I banged my head on.

I was in central Turkey and to achieve all of my goals I would have to get a move on so I took a big loop north and east passing through the capital of Ankara, then southeast to Uçhisar in Cappadocia. Cappadocia is a well-known tourist destination with its dramatic rock formations and 'Fairy Houses' cut into the rock.

The road south was good tarmac and I made swift progress back to the coast, then southeast to Antakya, a city that would be devastated by the earthquakes of 2022.

I was just north of the Syrian border and wanted to visit the site of Alexander's greatest battle on the banks of the Pinarus River near the town of Iskenderun. It was here on November 5, 333 BC that Alexander defeated the Persian Army led by Darius III. It was this victory that secured his conquest of Asia Minor.

My stay in Iskenderun coincided with the Kurban Bayrami. A rather bizarre celebration where families buy a sheep and parade the creature around on a lead, like a pet dog, then slit its throat. I was invited to join a family for the feast, but the smell put me off lamb for a couple of years.

By this stage, I had achieved my goal and was running a week late in the plan, so pointed the bonnet of Bucephalus west along the glorious coast road, then north up to Istanbul and a swift run home through Bulgaria and Romania.

My plan was nearly ruined at the border into Bulgaria as my visa had expired. Half an hour of friendly negotiations and a gift of $20 for the border guard to 'buy something for his children' seemed to open the barrier and I was away.

A day later I was in Budapest and remember noting that the last set of traffic lights as I left the city were on green. This seemed a good omen and the next set I encountered was in Dover when I disembarked the ferry 19 hours later. CLR

Pamukkale is a World Heritage Site formed by calcite-rich springs dripping slowly down the mountainside

On the banks of the Pinarus River where on 5th November 333 BC Alexander defeated the Persian Army led by Darius III. A battle that secured his conquest of Asia Minor